Windows

Into the Life of a Priest

by

Rev. Robert A. Lange

With a forward by Dr. Kenneth D. Whitehead

Loreto Publications
Fitzwilliam, NH 03447
A.D. 2013

ISBN: 978-1-62292-082-2

Loreto Publications
P. O. Box 603
Fitzwilliam, NH 03447
603–239–6671
www.loretopubs.org

Dedication

To the Blessed Virgin Mary

"Mary Reconciler of People and Nations"
under which title she made herself known at
Betania in Venezuela.

Acknowledgments

Allow me to take a moment to acknowledge and to thank those whose help, encouragement, and prayers have made my book a reality. If it were not for them, you would not be reading these pages.

At the outset, it must be recognized that the Blessed Virgin Mary prompted me to write, and that she has been looking over my efforts from their beginning to the present. For example, I received an e-mail from Loreto Publications on the feast of the Visitation stating that they would like to publish. Was it a mere coincidence that I received the great news that a publishing house with a deep Marian affiliation was interested in publishing my book? Not hardly. Again, on the feast of the Dedication of St. Mary Major, the oldest church in the world dedicated to the Virgin, I received notice from Loreto that pre-publication work should be completed by late September. Truly, Mother Mary has been there for me always. Thank you, Blessed Virgin Mary.

The first person to encourage me, other than my best friend and sister, Mary Lou, was Barbara Horn. She not only encouraged me even before I wrote the first words of the manuscript, but she volunteered to become its editor. Many stories could be told of the interchanges between me, the fledgling author, and the editor whose purpose was only to make my writing readable and acceptable.

Dr. Kenneth Whitehead and his lovely wife Margaret were supporters from day one also. Dr. Whitehead, who has been published many times, gave the me confidence to continue the process of writing and then pursuing publication. Both Ken and Margaret said that my story needed to be told. Ken also recommended Loreto Publications who accepted my manuscript.

Many former parishioners encouraged me with assurances of support, prayers, and best wishes. If I began to list all of these wonderful friends, I would be almost certain to inadvertantly leave some important person off of my list. All of you who deserve my thanks know who you are, and I do thank you from the bottom of my heart.

Of course I am deeply grateful to Loreto Publications for publishing my book. All publishers receive many manuscripts yearly, most of them are never published. To have mine accepted by them shows the confidence that they have in me. I am grateful.

Father Robert Lange

Contents

Foreword ix
Introduction xiii
Angels Earning their Wings 1
Under Mary's Mantle 13
Road to Priesthood 33
You Are a Priest Forever 61
Priesthood–A New Life Begins 77
Betania 95
Prayerful Thoughts and Images 125
A Final Glimpse 137
Appendix 145

Foreword

Father Robert A. Lange's engaging memoir, *Windows into the Life of a Priest*, supplies exactly what the book's title indicates, namely, an anecdotal account of one man's Catholic priesthood. While it is autobiographical in the sense that it is based largely on Father Lange's life and experiences as a priest, the aim and purpose of the book belong more to the realm of Catholic faith and devotion generally, and, indeed, to that of Catholic apologetics, giving reasons for the faith, offering "a defense . . . for the hope that is in [us]" (1 Pet 3:13). Among other things, Father Lange turns out to be quite an effective apologist for the faith.

At various times in the text, Father Lange remarks, in effect, that "It's not about *me*!" Rather, it's about faith and God's grace, how important and indeed necessary they are, and how they literally make life worth living. Father Lange certainly shows that they have made *his* life worth living—and worth recounting too, for the benefit of others, especially for those he calls wayward Christians. If God could save him—and by save here is meant not only eternal salvation, but rescue from an aimless and empty life here and now—why could he not save you or me as well? That, in fact, is precisely what God wants to do for all of us; he wants to save us from ourselves—if only you and I will respond to his love, abundantly offered to everyone, and cooperate! This is an important part of the message that Father Lange never tires of repeating.

The book is also about the Catholic priesthood to which Father Lange aspired, and that he attained. With God's help he overcame many shortcomings, difficulties, and traumas to become a priest. This is all recounted in loving detail in these pages. Father Lange reveres the priesthood, and treats it with a kind of awe even after all the years he himself has now been a priest.

As an author Father Lange presents himself, perhaps exaggeratedly, as a simple, down-to-earth average man, with, however, as he tells the story, more than average flaws, shortcomings, and brokenness. He was away from the faith for a number of years, living an aimless, undisciplined, and even sometimes dissolute life. He is quite frank about all this. Yet through a return to the faith of his childhood, and by God's grace, as he makes clear, he proved able to become a priest and a pastor in a position to help others in his turn, especially by orienting them towards the same faith in Jesus Christ, in his church, and in the graces that come from faithful Catholic practice and participation in the sacraments that he has experienced in his own life.

Just as the long pontificate of Blessed Pope John Paul II demonstrated again that any authentic Catholic faith is also necessarily Marian, so Father Lange is fervent in his devotion to the Blessed Virgin Mary, whom he believes has intervened in his life.

Father Lange, in short, quite simply believes that the Catholic faith is true. He believes this in a real and not merely in a notional sense. It is not something abstract; nor is it merely a philosophy, or a theory, or a habit; it is real. It is the truth. Similarly, miracles are real, he affirms, just as are also real interventions by God or by his holy angels, which Father believes he has experienced in his own life. In writing about all this, he also gets into describing various saints, devotions (especially to the Blessed Mother), apparitions, and other graced happenings. Almost painfully honest in describing the failures and traumas in his own life, he nevertheless often sees the pain of it all transformed into love and joy through faith. Written in a relaxed and readable style, the book successfully presents vignettes from this priest's life which are both interesting in themselves, and often edifying, though not in an overly preachy way.

At one point, Father Lange remarks: "If I had any gift, it was my sincerity . . . I speak from my heart." The same thing is true of this book as well; his sincerity indeed does come across. Once again, however, it is not about him. The "me generation" seems to have wholly by-passed him. Rather, his book is about Jesus Christ and his Blessed Mother and his church and how they change the lives of Christians daily—how they do, in fact, make life worth living.

Kenneth D. Whitehead

Introduction

On one of my priestly assignments there was a sidewalk that led from the rectory directly to the church sacristy, the room in the church where the priests put on their vestments for Mass and for other liturgical celebrations. If it rained more than a sprinkle, numerous worms would come to the surface to enjoy the moisture. They would be overcome with such delight that they would venture onto the sidewalk. At the beginning of their undertaking, there had been plenty of moisture to support their endeavor. However, when the rain stopped, the pools on the concrete would dry, leaving the poor worms away from their natural element and exposed to the harsh reality of death unless some Saint Francis-type person would pick them up and place them back in their natural habitat.

Our Lord's insight to me is that many times we imitate those foolish worms. Life has its false attractions, glittery distractions which draw our attention away from its true purpose. We venture away from God's grace to try life on our own, only to discover that life without Christ is no life at all. Spiritually, and sometimes physically, we begin to wither and die. Then along comes Our Lord, who through grace, picks us up and tries to return us to our natural environment. As he raises us from the sidewalk with his pierced hands we know he is helping us, but we are ungrateful and even bite his hands as he gently positions us where we will be better off.

I relate to those poor, dumb worms! "There go I except for the grace of God." Even with his unfailing love, I still end up on those proverbial sidewalks of death and destruction, which lead to sin. In my pride, arrogance, and selfishness I venture out on my own thinking, "I can handle this situation," only to find myself high and dry, alone and needing divine help to straighten my life out once again. The image I have of myself is of a worm that is forever trying to do things on its own, only to endlessly discover that this worm not only needs God merely to survive, but that its life would be much happier and more fulfilled in its own natural habitat—that is, living in the grace of the eternal God of love.

Focus! These pages are written to focus our attention on the abundant personal love that God has for each of us. In and out of season, we need to focus our attention on the true purpose of life; to get to heaven, and how God interacts with each of us in order to help us attain that goal.

Through all the years of our lives, God's love is a constant. It never wavers. It never decreases. Even if we do not feel his presence, seek his presence, or even care if he is present in our lives, he is there. Our Lord's purpose for creating us is so that we may be with him in heaven at the eternal banquet, which will be the fulfillment of all our hopes and desires, where we will understand that we are unconditionally loved as is.

I call myself a GP, a General Practitioner. I am not a holy person or a gifted speaker, nor am I the brightest light on the block. I wasted many years of my life by not practicing my faith. Yet God was always with me through those empty years, even though I was not with him, as he is with each one of us.

I am writing to give hope to all people, especially to those who see themselves as ordinary, and to those who suffer physical, emotional, and/or spiritual difficulties. I am writing to give hope to those who are depressed, to those who have no belief system, and to those who simply need encouragement. I deeply desire to give hope to those who feel inadequate in life, as well as to those who do not know that their lives do indeed have great meaning for our eternal, all-loving God. Even the most hidden or wretched of lives is precious to Our Lord.

To those who have no belief system and somehow, through God's will, come across these writings, my challenge to you is this: try to connect the dots of my life without the interaction of a personal God. It is impossible!

If we had a better understanding of the total picture of reality we would definitely understand that God is interacting in our lives at every moment. If we have not yet discovered this to be true, maybe these writings will help. I pray this will be so.

It is imperative for everyone to understand the supreme purpose for which God has made us, which is to get to heaven. However, in addition to this awesome goal, God gives meaning and purpose to daily living; each day should be precious to us. I will try to illustrate this point with accounts of a few manifestations of his love, which I have witnessed over the years.

Throughout my life, Our Lord has quietly worked miracle after miracle. Twice before I was thirteen years old, I was saved miraculously from certain death. I can count at least three times when I have experienced physical interaction with my guardian angel. I was given the gift of priesthood, despite having nothing to boast of myself, nor being in the slightest way deserving of it. In fact, I was so slow in responding to God's call to priesthood that he had to hit me in the head with a spiritual two-by-four in the form of a locution* and perform many miracles to foster the spiritual and emotional development I needed in order to become his priest. In the pages that follow, other miracles will be explored as well.

Most of the time we do not recognize miracles for what they are. We normally say we had a bit of good luck, or things happened by chance, or perhaps we had some good fortune, when in reality God was working little acts of love just for us, real miracles.

Angels Earning Their Wings

A Heavenly Nudge

Just before dusk one August evening in 1949, in Richmond, Virginia, my Mom got some of her children together and walked us down to the playground, a city park about two blocks from our home. Those were the days before air-conditioning, almost before television. We did have a primitive TV and were happy with our lone television station which made its home in Richmond. It was a time when most Americans still adhered to basic Christian morality, and a time when virtue was still admired and common decency was a given. We did not give a second thought to going out and walking around our own neighborhood at night in a large city.

Back then children, (only goats had kids according to Mom), might ask their mom or dad, “Hey, would it be alright if we went over Billy’s house for a while?” The response would probably be something like “Sure! Say hello to his parents for us and don’t wear out your welcome! Be back when the streetlights come on. Behave yourselves and have a good time!”

Children would roam the neighborhoods fearlessly, and without close parental supervision either. However that was not the way it was for me, not yet anyway. I was only five years old in 1949, just a bit too young for that kind of liberty. I was the youngest of six children (four girls and two boys), a bit spoiled, and life was great! What a different culture it was from today.

Well, back to the playground. It was a hot, starlit night with not a cloud in the sky. As with most August days in Richmond, we would have loved to have had a little thunderstorm. The temperature was in the upper 80s at least, and it was humid too. We didn't care; we were used to it and didn't know any differently.

Mother put me into one of those old-fashioned swings that had a bar in front to keep the kid, I mean the child, from falling out. So there I sat, swinging away, listening to the music blare over loud speakers, having a great time in the breeze of the swing. Mom was standing a short distance away with a few ladies, relaxing and talking a bit. All of a sudden my mother heard what she thought was a clap of thunder . . . but on a starlit night? Instinctively (nudged by an angel or by the Blessed Mother?) she ran over and grabbed me from the swing and brought me to where she and the other mothers were standing.

Within thirty seconds a huge tree came crashing down on the exact spot where I had been swinging, smashing to the ground the bars that supported the framework of the swings. I was almost killed! I probably didn't realize this at the time; rather I was just happy to be in the loving embrace of my mother. What kind of understanding does a five-year-old have of life or death anyway?

If we think about it, there are some wonderful lessons for life in this episode. First of all, the tree appeared to be perfectly healthy. It was between fifty to seventy-five years old, with a full growth of summer leaves. Looking at the tree no one would have ever thought that it was in danger of falling. It goes to show that it is not the outside that counts, but what is on the inside that really matters. That tree was rotten to the core and the thunder my mom heard was really the cracking of the trunk of the dead tree as it fell onto my swing.

This reminds me of the story of Dorian Gray, in which a man continues to look young, healthy, and wholesome, while his image in a picture becomes more decrepit over time, showing a true image of his soul. It also brings to mind an admonition of Saint Paul, who said that it was more important to work on internal cleanliness rather than on external observances of Jewish ceremonial purification. Christ says the same in the gospels, that it is what that comes out of the man that is impure. Then he gives a list of the sins that afflict the human person from within.

It is a doctrine of the church which says that each of us has at least one guardian angel looking after us. Some mystics say that they have seen people who have two or more angelic guardians. I do not know for sure, but because of some encounters with my own guardian angel later in life, my opinion is that it was that heavenly spirit who warned my mother to move me out of the swing.

We need to be grateful to our guardian angels and pray to God in appreciation of their work in our behalf. Many of us owe our very lives to them. Additionally, we need to recognize that when we sin, we disappoint our guardians making their jobs much more difficult.

What do you think regarding the tree that almost took my life? Was it a heavenly nudge or was it just a mother's instinct? Did my guardian angel tap my mother on the shoulder? Did the Blessed Mother urge my mom to act? To this day, I do not know for sure. Nevertheless, I do know that on a hot August night in 1949, at the age of five, I was saved from death because my mother moved me from that baby swing just before that tree came crashing down. That is a fact.

Why was my life spared? Why me? It was years into priesthood before I realized that my life had been spared that evening. What was the purpose of my surviving the crashing down of that tree? I still ask myself how am I to respond properly to being spared.

Did God simply want to give me another chance at life? Was there something he had in mind for me? Did an evil being know of God's plan and cause that tree to fall to try to foil Our Lord's intention? Many possibilities have run through my mind. What I do know is that I must be grateful. I try to show my gratitude by attempting to understand life, as well as my little role in it, and by responding with greater love. We should realize that God's love is infinite for each of us. I have been shown that time and time again. If we reflect sufficiently on our lives with this in mind, I am certain that we all have been shown his immeasurable love. As for me, I know that I must respond by directing my life towards drawing ever closer to him and by trying to live so as to bring others to him.

What a noble and wonderful a vocation we have: to be disciples of Jesus Christ, living in this world but with our mind and heart set on the next. It is a vocation for each of us! I often wonder why it took so long for that simple truth, and the beauty of that truth, to sink in. Was I simply being thickheaded, or was I just distracted by the false glitz of this world?

All of us are protected in many ways by our guardian angels, although we are not aware of it most of the time. There is a wonderful series of books by Joan Wester Anderson written on the subject of angels' actions in the lives of ordinary people. These books are narratives of how our angelic bodyguards keep us safe, physically and spiritually, all through our lives.

A friend of mine, who jogs regularly, related to me a lifesaving incident regarding his guardian angel. He was in a residential neighborhood, jogging down a sidewalk, when he heard a distinct voice within that said, "STOP!" He did stop at once just as a car that had been hidden by a hedge suddenly backed out of a driveway and into the street, only about two steps in front of him. The driver screeched to a halt, rolled down the window, and expressed apologies to my buddy. Both realized that if my friend had not stopped dead in his tracks at that exact moment, there was a great possibility that he would have been killed. Was it my friend's guardian angel who told him to stop? No other explanation is plausible.

Seek that relationship with your guardian angel. Ask for his help. Thank him for looking over you. Ask him his name. Ask to see him. Ask to hear him more clearly. Give thanks to God for his many ways of looking after you. Glory in his love and care for you.

Blessed Pope John XXIII, the great pontiff who called for an ecumenical council which resulted in Vatican II, would send his guardian angel on special missions. When he had a difficult meeting coming up, he would send his guardian angel on ahead of him to speak to the other attendees' guardian angels in order to soften them up, to make them more amenable to whatever he wanted to discuss with them.

Our guardian angels want to be used by us. They want to have missions. They desire to help us in any way that they can. Let's take advantage of their ability to aid us in our earthly life. We should form personal bonds with them, and make them an integral part of our lives.

Putting My Guardian Angel to the Test

The summer of 1956 was a much simpler time when I remember going most of the summer without putting on shoes, except to go to Mass. Drug stores had soda fountains where you could order a Cherry Coke mixed right in front of you. Scenes from 1956 might remind some people of the movie Back to the Future. That movie was fantasy, but what I have to relate is fact and is a marvelous reminder of how Our Lord is looking out for us every day. My guardian angel was the instrument that God used to show his love for me that particular day.

I can remember the details of that tragic but miraculous morning as if it were yesterday. Perhaps that is because I still wear a boomerang-shaped scar on my right forearm. The scar is about six and one-half inches long and reminds me of that unforgettable day.

Every year from my third birthday through my eighteenth, our family would go to the river. Those fifteen summers were idyllic and memorable. Dad would rent a cottage for us to enjoy from mid-June through mid-July, for four to five weeks at a time! There was one exception to this idyllic life and boys, being boys, caused that.

What was the river? It could have been one of dozens of rivers that flow through Virginia. Going to the river was the way many of the middle-class in central Virginia vacationed in those days, and still do. In our case the river was the lower Potomac on the Virginia side, Sandy Point to be exact.

The cottage had no air conditioning or central heating, no television, no telephone, and of course none of the other modern conveniences that we have come to expect now in the third millennium. However, we had a wonderful time there! The boys slept in a dorm room on old WWII army cots, while the girls enjoyed real beds in semi-private rooms. Many of our cousins and friends were there! Sometimes we would have fifteen people staying there weekdays, and on weekends our numbers would almost double. I am glad I didn't have to do the cooking!

We spent our time on the beach, in the water, or puttering around in our twelve-foot boat, which was powered by a twenty-horsepower engine. Evenings were spent playing card games, charades, or board games like Scrabble. Rainy days meant sitting on the screened porch, boys picking on the girls, listening to rock 'n' roll on a 45 rpm single-play record player, and wishing for the sunshine to return so we could jump back in the water, go fishing, throw horseshoes, or maybe put together a game of softball.

Getting back to that eventful day: Dad had just bought Mom her first new car, a 1956 blue-on-blue Chevrolet Bel-Air, four-door sedan. There was no air-conditioning of course, not even an AM radio. What it did have was a V-8 engine with a three-speed stick shift on the column. That car was fast! Dad was at home in Richmond while Mom, her new car, and her teenage boys were at Sandy Point!

On that fateful morning about a week into our vacation, we boys (including my brother, five years my senior, his buddy, a cousin who was three years older than me, and myself) decided to ride down the road a mile or so to swim. It was the same river, and the same beach, so perhaps the attraction was to get away from parental supervision, to be out on our own, or something like that.

That was when the trouble began, as my brother and his friend got into the car. To be annoying, as siblings typically will do, they would not let my cousin and me get in, so my cousin suggested that he and I ride on the hood of the car. Imagine two boys, one twelve and the other fifteen, wearing only bathing suits, not even shoes or shirts, sitting on the front of a moving car. Oh yes, we did have our inner tubes (early forms of flotation devices) with us as we jumped onto the hood of that '56 Chevy.

My brother squealed out as my cousin and I looked at each other with fear written on our faces, recognizing at once that we had made a big mistake. Everything happened so fast! I had nothing to hold onto! We threw the inner tubes off, and my cousin grabbed the hood ornament to help him keep his balance, leaving me with nothing to grasp. Then he jumped off the side of the car and rolled unharmed into the grassy ditch.

I guess I panicked! I remember being off-balance, scared, and being tossed back and forth by the motion of the car, as my brother threw it into second gear or as the brakes were being applied. The next thing I knew I was suspended in mid-air, hanging in front of the car as it slowed down. I never hit the ground until the car came to a full stop!

The hood ornament had hooked my right forearm! There was a huge hole in my arm. However, the hood ornament had held me off the ground until the car stopped moving. When a doctor finally attended to it, he put seventeen stitches on the inside of the wound and eleven more on the outside. Today, more than fifty-five years later, I can still see and count the marks the stitches left on my arm.

What are the odds of surviving a forward fall from the hood of a fast-moving car? Yet that is exactly what happened. If the hood ornament had not snagged my arm, I would have fallen in front of the grill of a moving vehicle, which was going fast enough to have killed me instantly.

The odds continued to be against me that day, but I defied them in two more incredible ways. First of all, according to the physician who stitched up the wound, if the cut had been only one-eighth of an inch deeper, a surgeon would have had to amputate my arm at the elbow. Secondly, there was a good chance that I would have bled to death even before I got to the doctor, if my brother-in-law had not been staying at the cottage that week. He knew how to apply a tourniquet to stop the massive bleeding. It was about twenty miles to the country doctor's house, and after arriving there we had to wait a long while to see him. Doc was in another town delivering a baby. The closest hospital was another hour or more away.

Count them, three miracles in one accident! Did I say I must have been living a blessed life? Indeed!

At the time, everyone in the family recognized that falling off a moving car was a terrible thing, and that it might have led to something far more serious than a terrifying gash on the arm. The way I see it now is that I was saved from certain death that day. Even so, I do not remember hearing the incident being spoken of after the initial frenzy. It has only been within the past few years that my brother and I have talked about it. He let me know only then that he had nightmares for a year after the accident.

As for me, it took entering the seminary in 1982, to study for Catholic priesthood, for me to begin deeply reflecting upon my life, God's intervention in it, and how blessed my entire life has been. It gradually came to me, probably five to ten years after my ordination, that my life was miraculously saved that July day back in 1956. (Being from the South, I take time to come to certain understandings, you know.) Reflecting on this amazing event of failing to hit the ground after falling face first off the front of that moving vehicle, and being saved from certain death, is just too much for words.

Here I am, more than twenty-six years into priesthood, asking myself, "How can I respond properly to such an intervention?" Although I still do not have a satisfying answer to that question, I do try to respond by being grateful and by recognizing that my life was given back to me that day. I am left with a desire to entrust my life, as well as my death, to God for his disposal, and to be used as he pleases. He saved me from death twice before I was thirteen years old. I feel that he purchased my life and death, physically and spiritually, not only with the death of his Son, Jesus Christ, but also through the tree and the car miracles. I am yours my God. Do with me as you wish.

Scripture says, "God is love." (1 Jn. 4:8) Scripture does not lie, according to Saint Robert Bellarmine. My life's experiences, preceding priesthood and since ordination, have confirmed these truths to me many times over. Everything that happens in our lives is for our good. God desires and does indeed draw good out of any and all situations in our lives, if we are open to him. The good, the bad, and the ugly all go into making us into the persons we become over time.

Our God is a personal God. He wants to be involved in our lives, but sometimes he needs to use tough love. Often people misinterpret his necessary approach as being judgmental, condemning, aloof, uncaring, or just uninvolved. All we need to do when we think that our heavenly Father does not love us is take some time for an active meditation on one of two events recorded in scripture: Jesus in the crib in Bethlehem, or Jesus dying on the cross on Calvary.

What do I mean by active meditation? Well, we can place ourselves into the actual event as it is happening. I do not mean imagining a photograph or a movie running in front of our minds. Rather, we actually become a part of the scene of scripture as it unfolds. For instance, we can place ourselves on Calvary, maybe at a distance from the actual crucifixion of Jesus, and begin to look around, observing the drunken Roman solders throwing dice for the garments of Jesus. Observe the crowds and see some people mocking Jesus as well as others who are crying for him. We might walk closer to Jesus dying on the cross, and see his labored efforts to pull himself up simply to breathe, the excruciating pain he feels, his determination to be faithful to the Father, and the lack of any anger in his pain-twisted face. We can observe the Blessed Mother and John the Apostle, their agony and their reactions to all that is happening. We can witness Jesus speaking to Mary and John, when he gives us his Mother to be our Mother. Then perhaps we can allow Jesus' eyes to catch ours. That will be an intimate moment!

Perhaps we can touch the cross and feel the blood on our fingers as it flows out of Our Lord's mangled and wounded body. We should take our time, ponder, and allow all the emotions, the reality, and the meaning to be absorbed not just in our brains, but also in our hearts, so that it becomes a part of us. If we understand these realities in our hearts, they will in turn help us in our daily struggles. The same method may be used with any scripture passage. This is one of the beautiful ways scripture should be read.

Can we imagine the eternal Word of God, the second person of the Blessed Trinity, who has no beginning and no end, who is all-powerful, who is the being through whom all creation was made, and who ". . . shared our human nature in all things but sin," even to being born in a filthy stable? Well, that is the reality of it!

This is a great meditation on God's absolute love for us, and of his profound humility. It might also remind us to consider how futile is the accumulation of material goods here on earth, and direct us toward becoming single-minded in trying to achieve our heavenly goal. Which is, after all, the whole purpose of Jesus' life on earth.

Meaningful meditations on the above historical interventions in human history by the Son of God will lead us to trust and love him intimately. I believe that if we look back at our lives, we will see touches of God's love in them. If we embrace these insights, these proofs of God's love for us, they will enable us to rise above the daily grind and to better seek our true home in heaven.

When I have a dark day, or more than one, I try to sit before Jesus in the Blessed Sacrament and reflect on the great acts of love Our Lord has worked in my life. I consider the major ones as well as the minor ones. The major act would of course be his Incarnation, as well as all the events that led up to and included the Pascal Mystery itself. The minor acts of love would be those that he has performed just for me, those daily coincidences that helped things work out well, like the sunset that reminded me of a special moment, and of course being saved from death as a child. Minor?

These insights and the awareness of his love played out in my daily life raise my mind and heart above the fog and rain to realize the temporary nature of all things here on earth. In reality, the only things that are permanent in our lives are God's love for us as individuals, and his unwavering efforts to help us understand this. his deep desire is for us to say "Yes!" to him so that we are enabled to enter into an ever-deepening union with him.

Under Mary's Mantle

Immediately after the Baptism, the priest took the newborn boy into his arms and walked over to the church's Marian altar. Father laid the infant on the altar, looked up at the image of the Virgin Mary over the altar and said, "He is yours." From that moment on, the Virgin placed her mantle of protection over that baby boy. The positive effects of the consecration of the baby to the Mother of God would continue throughout the boy's life and prove to be an exceedingly significant act.

I was that infant and the priest dedicated me to the Mother of God for her special protection in good times and in bad, whether I wanted her mantle over me or not. I was named after the priest who performed the Baptism that day, as well as for the saint upon whose feast day I was born.

What a gift! I was named after the great Saint Anthony of Padua, named in honor of a living priest and dedicated to the Blessed Virgin Mary! Truly, nothing has greater value than receiving the sacrament of Baptism. These were such special blessings to be bestowed upon anyone, and I was less than a month old.

As Jesus hung dying on the cross for us, one of his last acts in this life was to give his mother a special apostolate—a never-ending task and one that many would call a thankless job. The apostle John records in his gospel narrative the whole incident. "When Jesus saw his mother, and the disciple whom he loved standing near, he said to his mother, 'Woman, behold your son!' Then he said to his disciple, 'Behold, your mother!' And from that hour the disciple took her to his own home." (Jn. 19:26–27)

This directive from Our Lord made it official. From that moment on, the Blessed Mother became our Mother evermore to intercede for us before the throne of her son, Jesus Christ. Jesus gave her a maternal interest in us. Of course she had been interceding for us all along. Who can forget her mediation on behalf of the newlyweds at the marriage feast of Cana? It was quite spectacular! At the same celebration she also gave us words to live by when she told the waiters, "Do whatever he tells you." (Jn. 2:5)

We address Mary by many glorious titles, as well we should. Who else is the Daughter of the Eternal Father, the Mother of his Son, and the Spouse of the Holy Spirit? Mary has the privilege of a personal and intimate relationship with each member of the Trinity. It would be to our detriment not to recognize how extraordinary Mary is and that she truly cares for each of us as her own. We should try to nurture our relationship with her. Mary desires that we do.

If we look back at Cana for a moment we will see Jesus beginning his public ministry ahead of time, simply to satisfy his mother. Jesus said to her "My hour has not yet come."(Jn. 2:4) He changed the timetable of his public ministry for her. Additionally, Mary's asking Jesus to intercede for the newly married couple shows a profound love for us. She knew that his time had not come, and that once he showed his mastery over nature, that act would start the clock ticking towards his death. Mary's love for mankind is so expansive that she was willing to start the ticking. Are these not concrete examples of an intimate loving relationship between God and his mother, and for us, too? Their relationship continues through time, keeps on bearing good fruit, and will continue eternally.

As his passion and death approached, Jesus told his apostles that he would not leave them orphaned. He promised to send the Paraclete, the Counselor, the Holy Spirit, to guide them into all truth. Both the New Testament and church tradition flow from the same source, the Holy Spirit. Both sacred scripture and church tradition show that Mary, the Mother of God, plays a necessary and prominent role in salvation history. Mary is a necessary tool in God's divine plan to bring us to salvation.

The Old and New Testaments are full of allusions to, and direct commentaries on, the Blessed Mother. For purposes here, I will focus on some of Mary's interactions with her children as witnessed mostly through church tradition. However, without knowing both scripture and tradition, it is impossible to have a balanced or full appreciation of the Mother of God, our Mother. (For those who would like a very readable commentary on Mary's role from scripture, I recommend *Hail, Holy Queen* by Dr. Scott Hahn.)

Tradition has it that Jesus appeared to his Mother in the year 40 A.D., several years after his own death, while she was living in Ephesus with the apostle John. Jesus' request was that she go to Spain in order to bolster the spirit of his cousin, the apostle James, who was having a most difficult time trying to convert the people of the Iberian Peninsula to the faith.

While Saint James was praying for strength with his disciples by the River Ebro, he happened to look up and saw (I am sure to his great surprise and maybe a little fright) a host of angels carrying the Blessed Mother on a five-foot pillar made of jasper. She spoke to James about his mission there in Spain as well as about his coming martyrdom back in Jerusalem.

According to the Blessed Mother's request, the site of her visitation to Saint James has been encapsulated in a basilica built in her honor. Called the Basilica of Our Lady of the Pillar, located in Zaragoza, it is the oldest shrine in the world dedicated to the Mother of God. The feast day of her visitation is celebrated on October 12. Our Lady told James that the shrine would remain there until the end of time for all who seek her intercession.

Even today, the shrine in Zaragoza continues to be the scene of many physical, emotional, and spiritual miracles. To show appreciation to the Virgin, many Spanish parents name their daughters Pilar (Spanish for pillar), in honor of Our Lady's visit to Spain two thousand years ago.

Christopher Columbus was a good Italian Catholic who sailed under the flag of the Spanish Queen, Isabella. The year was 1492, and Columbus' first voyage was underway in an attempt to discover the New World. He had been at sea for many months in those three small ships, one being named the Santa Maria in honor of the Virgin Mary. His men were beginning to mutiny, never a good sign. Columbus was discouraged himself. He found himself praying to the Virgin, and she answered his call. Shortly thereafter he set foot on land in the New World for the first time. The date? October 12th! Coincidence? It is the same date that the Spanish celebrate Our Lady of the Pillar.

Our Lady of the Pillar was there to help Saint James the apostle to bring the beginnings of Christianity to Spain. More than fourteen hundred years later she was there to help Spain bring Christianity to the New World. In God's eyes there are no coincidences! Our Lady's maternal interests for us, her children, are evident in every age. Our Lady of the Pillar loves you.

Before going any further, we need to look briefly at two more scripture passages. The first is from the book of Genesis, the first book in the Bible. An incident occurred immediately after God the Father had banished Adam and Eve from the Garden of Eden for eating from the forbidden tree. Our Father is speaking to Satan, the devil. The woman referred to is the Blessed Virgin Mary. This passage is considered to be the first hint of good news for mankind, the first gospel. This is where the Father begins to hint at his plan for salvation history.

"I will put enmities between thee and the woman, and thy seed and her seed: she_shall crush thy head, and thou shalt lie in wait for her heel . . . " (Gen. 3:15) This image is a favorite of painters and sculptors throughout Western culture. My grade school classrooms had images of the Virgin crushing the head of the serpent. I always found the head of the serpent to be scary, yet I was much impressed by the Lady with the gentle face who crushed it. Yea!

We have already seen in the Gospel of John how Our Lord has given us his Mother to be our Mother. Now let us look at the last book of sacred scripture, the book of Revelation.

"And a great sign appeared in the heaven, a woman clothed with the sun, with the moon under her feet, and on her head a crown of twelve stars, and being with child she cried, travailing in birth, and was in pain to be delivered. And there was seen another sign in heaven: and behold a great red dragon, having seven heads, and ten horns: and on his heads seven diadems. And his tail drew the third part of the stars of heaven, and cast them to the earth: and the dragon stood before the woman who was ready to be delivered; that, when she should be delivered, he might devour her son, and she brought forth a man child, who was to rule all nations with an iron rod: and her son was taken up to God, and to his throne. And the woman fled into the wilderness, where she had a place prepared by God, that there they should feed her a thousand two hundred sixty days."(Apoc. 12:1–6)

Have you seen the image of Our Lady of Guadalupe? The likeness described by John in the Apocalypse written during the late first century A.D., perfectly describes Our Lady's image depicted in her apparitions to Blessed Juan Diego in Guadalupe (Mexico City) in 1531, fifteen hundred years later.

One of Spain's primary reasons for exploring the New World was to convert the natives to the Catholic faith and to make the sacraments available to them so they would enjoy a supernatural relationship with Our Lord in the world to come.

Spanish solders marched into what is now Mexico City as a conquering army in 1519. Franciscan and Jesuit missionaries, whose goal was the conversion of the natives, went with them. Yet some twelve years later, few inroads had been made into the vicious and bloody practices of the Aztecs, who offered human sacrifices to their gods. Thousands and thousands were killed in these horrible pagan rituals. Mel Gibson's movie Apocalypto does justice in exposing the true nature of this bloodthirsty culture that the Spanish missionaries encountered upon their arrival in Mexico.

Juan Diego was the only visionary of Our Lady of Guadalupe. On one of her apparitions, the Virgin left an image of herself on his tilma, an overcoat. This is the only instance in two thousand years from which we have a true likeness of the Mother of God as she appeared to a visionary. That is historic!

How did it all happen? It is a great story within a story involving a humble peasant who was trying to avoid contact with Mary. Nevertheless, once confronted and "forced" into her service, Juan Diego dutifully and persistently carried out Mary's wishes.

In December of 1531, the Blessed Mother appeared to Juan Diego and instructed him to tell the local bishop to have a temple (church) built in her honor on the spot known as Tepeyac, which was the location of an abandoned temple built to honor a false female deity. Imagine the fear and trepidation of Juan Diego, a poor peasant, upon being charged by the Blessed Mother to approach a bishop.

When the bishop did not heed Our Lady's words relayed to him by Juan Diego, she became more forceful. The next time Juan Diego passed by Tepeyac, the Virgin Mary was waiting with new instructions. He was to take roses, which she had personally handpicked, to the bishop with the instructions to give them to no one else! The Virgin not only picked the roses but also helped Juan arrange them in the tilma.

Juan Diego complied. He went to the bishop's residence and asked to see His Excellency, the bishop. For over three hours, Juan was ridiculed and humiliated by the bishop's attendees because of his visions of Mary. Now Juan was determined to follow the Virgin's orders no matter the cost.

Finally, the bishop granted Juan Diego an audience. History changed forever when Juan Diego opened his tilma, displaying the roses which were sent by the Virgin Mary! What is more, to Juan Diego's own astonishment and to the surprise and delight of everyone in the room, there for all to behold was the awesome image of Our Lady painted on the tilma that we now recognize as Our Lady of Guadalupe!

The bishop recognized the roses as native to Castile, in Spain. Freshly picked Castilian roses, in Mexico, in mid-December? Impossible! The solution to the puzzle of the presence of these roses had to be heaven's intervention. Finally, Our Lady had the bishop's attention! This was confirmation, a proof that Juan Diego had been truthful and that Virgin Mary was serious about her request for a new church to be built in her honor.

This image of Our Lady is spectacular for many reasons. First of all, it exists! That is primary. The image shows Our Lady as described in scripture in the Book of the Apocalypse, which was composed fifteen hundred years earlier. In the image, she is standing on the moon, is clothed with the sun—actually blocking out the sun—and has a crown of twelve stars on her head. She is also with child, showing herself to be a mother.

The Aztecs worshiped the moon, and Our Lady in the image is standing on it! She is standing in front of the sun, actually blocking it out. The Aztecs worshiped the sun also. Therefore the Aztecs concluded that Our Lady must be greater than either the moon or the sun. However she could not be a god because she has her head bowed in prayer. Additionally, she shows respect for the unborn because she is with child.

Our Lady of Guadalupe, the image on the tilma, is an icon for all peoples, for all ages. This single image led to the conversion of all Mexico in only five years. Eight million natives were baptized during that period. Our Lady saved her children from violent physical death, (human sacrifice) and gave them a supernatural relationship with Our Lord through Baptism. She cares for her children in every age.

Because of her concern for God's children we have, marked in time forever, the exact likeness of how the Mother of God appeared in 1531 to the people of Mexico. What a gift this is! It is there for all to see, a portrait of the Virgin Mary on a piece of cloth made from the cactus plant.

One hundred and fifty years after the apparition, the image was brought inside, to better care for it. It took that long for the custodians of the image to understand that it needed to be protected from the elements. It should be preserved for future generations. It is priceless! It is an image of Jesus' mother.

A tilma is made of cactus, a fiber which has a life expectancy of twenty years at most. Yet almost five hundred years later this tilma still stands as a beautiful reminder that the Mother of Jesus loves her people with a burning maternal love. In the 1920s, the anti-Catholic regime that ruled Mexico tried to destroy the image with explosives. They were unsuccessful, of course. Most everything around the image was destroyed, but not the tilma. Divine intervention? Yes, indeed!

Scientists have studied the image but are unable to ascertain what paint was used to create it. They have magnified the eyes of the image and have discovered the reflection of the people who were in the room when Juan Diego unfolded the tilma for the bishop. Also, the stars on the garment worn by Our Lady show the heavens with the stars positioned as they were the evening when she appeared. It is of heavenly origin and only God has the answers as to the how and why of all of these mysteries.

Additionally, Our Lady of Guadalupe stands as a beautiful pro-life image for the world. The image is a silent reflection of why we should develop a devotion to the preborn Christ, who spent nine months in the virginal womb of the Virgin Mary. By doing so, he sanctified all wombs and confirmed, once and for all, the sacredness of motherhood.

This apparition of Our Lady of Guadalupe brings into sharp focus the battle between Our Blessed Mother (the woman crushing the head of Satan, the woman clothed with the sun) and the ancient serpent. Our Lady is a central figure in the battle against the devil. In our daily battles with evil, we would do well to invoke the Virgin Mary to assist us. She is the devil's primary adversary. By invoking Our Lady, we will overcome evil and attain virtue, making us more pleasing in Jesus' eyes. Our Lady of Guadalupe loves you.

Once again, moving ahead a few years, we turn our attention back to Europe. In 1571, just forty years after Our Lady appeared in Mexico to Juan Diego, Europe was in grave danger of falling under the control of the Ottoman Empire, the forces of Islam.

On October 7, 1571, the Catholic forces of Europe engaged in battle on the waters of the Mediterranean against overwhelmingly superior forces of the Turkish fleet. While the Catholic forces had 212 ships, the Ottomans had 286. Down in the bowels of their ships, the Turkish fleet was powered by thousands of Catholic slaves.

Pope Saint Pius V called upon all Europe to ask Our Lady's intercession against the superior enemy forces by praying the Rosary for victory. Additionally, Andrea Doria, one of three admirals commanding the Catholic forces, had a small image of Our Lady of Guadalupe that he carried into battle that day. At the height of the battle, when all seemed lost for the Catholic forces, Admiral Doria went to his stateroom and prayed before the image of Our Lady of Guadalupe. She answered his urgent prayers, and you can now see that same image enshrined in the Church of San Stefano in Aveto, Italy, as a memento of the great victory won that day by the Blessed Mother.

It was an overwhelming victory for the Catholic forces! While the Catholics lost fifty galleys and suffered about thirteen thousand casualties, the Ottomans lost 210 ships, twenty-five thousand killed, and many more thousands were taken as prisoners. The Catholic forces freed almost as many slaves from the Turks (about thirteen thousand) as they had lost soldiers and sailors in battle, thus offsetting their casualties.

Beyond doubt this was the decisive battle for the control of the Mediterranean Sea, which thus stopped invasion of

Europe by hostile Islamic fundamentalists. Because of the intercession of the Mother of God, through her powerful Rosary, and her image as Our Lady of Guadalupe, we are free to practice our Catholic faith today. Our Lady of Victory loves you.

These historical events from human history clearly show Our Lady's maternal concern for her people. Mothers will always go that extra mile, not only to see their children survive, but to help them achieve a better life. How much more is this true of the Mother of God.

The Virgin Mother has been given incredible gifts. She was immaculately conceived; that is, she was conceived without original sin. Our Lady was redeemed by the same salvific act of Jesus as all of us have been, but she received the graces of that act ahead of time, as a foretaste of the great sacrificial act accomplished by her Son, Jesus Christ.

The interventions in human history by our spiritual Mother also show the incredible influence that she possesses with the Godhead as an intercessor, as demonstrated in John's gospel account of the wedding feast at Cana. The guests at the wedding reception were clueless that they were witnessing the first of what has become a continuous line of intercessions, by Mary, for her children. The relationship between Mary and her divine Son is so strong, loving, and integral to the Father's salvific plan for us that it is impossible for us to grasp its depth and importance. It will continue to be felt at least until the second coming of Jesus.

These accounts which are spoken of in scripture (Gen. 3:15 and Apoc. 12:17) also plainly demonstrate that Mary has been given divine authority over evil, and that she does battle with the ancient serpent constantly, persistently, and relentlessly. In addition, they show us who is the ultimate victor of this warfare. Having to do battle with a woman is an extra humiliation for Satan. The Blessed Virgin Mary loves you.

I have barely scratched the surface in the volumes of evidence that are available regarding the Blessed Mother's involvement in the daily lives of her children. Every country and every age has numerous and beautiful accounts of her deep abiding love for us. I will mention several more examples.

It was the middle of the night in Paris when a youthful looking angel awakened a novice of the Daughters of Charity, Sr. Catherine Labouré. He announced to her that the Mother of God requested her presence in the convent chapel at once. Upon entering the chapel, Catherine reverenced the Blessed Sacrament then heard the rustle of silk, and turned to see a blinding light. The light took the form of the Blessed Mother, who was sitting in the celebrant's chair. (My heart would have been beating out of my body, in ecstasy!)

The Virgin Mary spent two hours with Catherine. It was an intimate experience for the novice as she laid her head on Mother Mary's lap and confided to her all the problems a young nun might have. For her part, the Blessed Mother stroked Catherine's hair as she listened to her daughter, giving Catherine reassurance that everything in her life would work itself out.

Catherine's life was one of obscurity caring for the least of God's children, even to the cleaning of lavatories in hostels for homeless men for many years. No one in her convent knew that she was the visionary responsible for having the Immaculate Conception Medal struck, per the Blessed Mother's instructions. Our Lady commissioned Catherine to have the medal made in order to provide protection for all who would wear it. It later became known as the Miraculous Medal.

What impresses me is the personal interest the Mother of God has in her children. I am awed by the Blessed Mother's love for each one of us demonstrated by her time and compassion shown to Saint Catherine in the chapel that fateful night in 1830. To think the Mother of God cares enough for us to sit and listen to our simple problems and to stroke our heads and hair. Such love is incredible.

This is not the whole story of the Miraculous Medal. Far from it! The medal is called miraculous because of the many miracles associated with those who wear it. I have found many accounts of healings, lives being physically saved, and conversions to the faith, from people who had the medal on their person. There are even accounts of these miraculous stories which have happened in our own times on You-Tube, the internet address familiar to millions of people world-wide. Our Lady of the Miraculous Medal loves you.

Pope John Paul II was gunned down in Saint Peter's Square on May 13, 1981. The professional assassin asserted that it was impossible that the pope could survive his assassination. He was positive that the bullet pierced the pope's heart. He was a professional. The Blessed Mother had other plans.

The pope was very seriously injured and should have died. However, the surgeons reported that the bullet entered the chest cavity of the Holy Father and went around the vital organs, missing them all. John Paul states that he was positive that the Blessed Mother, Our Lady of Fatima, to be exact, guided the bullet so it would do the least harm to her pope. From that moment, the Holy Father entered into a special and profound relationship with Our Lady of Fatima. May 13th happened to be the anniversary of the first apparition of the Blessed Mother at Fatima, in Portugal, to three children. Some say the date was coincidence, but that was not the opinion of the Holy Father.

The Blessed Mother's third secret given to the children at Fatima concerned a "pope that had to suffer much." John Paul? Possibly. John Paul had a very strong devotion to Our Lady. He had consecrated his life and his pontificate to her. His motto *Totus Tuus* (All Yours) referred to his love and devotion to/for the Mother of God. His commitment to Our Lady came after reading and digesting True Devotion to Mary by Saint Louis de Montfort. The Holy Father was convinced that since Christ comes to us through Mary, we need to go to Christ through her.

John Paul II recognized the sacred scripture passages pertaining to the Virgin and saw the continual intercessions Mary has had throughout the history of the church. He saw her as a great mediator, the Mother of God's children, a model of the church, and a fierce opponent of the ancient serpent. He saw her also as a primary weapon in God's arsenal to put the devil back into hell for good. John Paul II was right on all of these points. Our Lady, Mother of the Church, loves you.

There are two things I know and believe regarding the Blessed Virgin Mary, which should involve God's people. All parents should have their children consecrated to Our Lady at their infants' Baptism, and everyone should make the de Montfort consecration to Mary as adults, with annual renewals. We should do everything possible to have a positive relationship with Jesus' Mother.

The Mother of God, Mary Most Holy, is our Mother and desires a personal relationship with each of us. Some say "I go directly to Jesus," or "I don't need Mary". Others actually make fun of her as being some sweet little Jewish girl who was used by God for a short period of time to simply bring his Son into the world. They hold her as counting for nothing. Stop being a stumbling block! Allow Mary into your life. You will be richer for it.

I have no qualms admitting that without Mary, my life would have probably ended, either at the age of five, in the swing in a city park, or at the age of twelve, by falling off the front of a car. Being consecrated to the Virgin does not give us license to do stupid things with the presumption that she will pull us through. But she does shower those who consecrate themselves to her with singular graces helping them overcome life's difficulties, thereby achieving holiness of life. If we ask, she will always respond.

One last word about the de Montfort consecration to Mary: when we make the consecration, we give our lives for her use. We give her our prayers and good works, our sufferings and our pains, our joys and accomplishments. We trust our persons to her, our lives and our deaths to her, all to be used as she wishes in the fight to bring more people to the heavenly banquet. By doing so, we become important members of God's army helping to bring about his triumphant reign as Christ the King.

To be a servant of the Mother of God is a sacred and beautiful calling, a mission to which we all should respond. By consecrating our lives to Mary, they take on a deeper meaning, a broader significance. Our lives and our actions have eternal consequences and unfathomable depths. Dying to self is mandatory. We begin to live not just for ourselves or even for our families, but for mankind. We become members of her army to help "crush the head of the ancient serpent."

Now that would be life in its fullness! Our Lady of Tenderness loves you!

The battle between David and Goliath happened a thousand years before the birth of the Blessed Virgin Mary, but there is a powerful connection between the battle and the Blessed Mother. We will explore that connection now.

David was a youth of ruddy complexion and probably small in stature, compared to the giant Goliath. A battle-hardened veteran with many kills to his credit, Goliath had nothing but contempt for this youth whom the Israelites sent out to do battle with him. David did not wear any armor when he went to battle Goliath; it did not fit and made his movements slow and cumbersome. Picture, if you will, this youth walking onto the battlefield, between two opposing armies, clad as a shepherd. Across the field from him was a huge, fierce warrior, fully clad in armor, yelling obscenities at David as they moved ever closer for combat. The closer they came to one another, the ever more apparent it became that David had no chance against this Philistine brute.

But wait! David reached into his pocket where he had five smooth stones. He took one of them out and placed it in his slingshot. The stone came out of his slingshot and hit Goliath squarely in his forehead, between his eyes, with such a force that it knocked the brute down and out cold. David approached the giant and dispatched him with Goliath's own sword! Battle over! Good defeated evil! Unmistakably, God was with David in his victory over Goliath. How else could a youth armed only with a slingshot and five stones defeat a fierce warrior like Goliath?

With our Rosaries in our pockets, we carry potent weapons in our fight against evil. The Rosary's five decades correspond directly to the five smooth stones David carried. We are at war just as David was, not with Goliath, a physical enemy, but with the forces of evil, our spiritual enemy. We defeat evil in our lives through the use of the sacraments and the Rosary. Many of the greatest saints of the modern church declare that when we pray the Rosary, we employ our greatest weapon against sin that exists, outside of the sacraments.

The human mind operates on two or more levels all the time. This fact is taken into account when we pray this ancient and venerable prayer to Mary, our Mother. We occupy the surface, or the more superficial part of our minds when we say the Hail Mary, while the deeper part of our being meditates on sacred scripture, the passages relating to events in the lives of Jesus and Mary. The meditation increases our understanding of these salvific events, which in turn draws us into a closer relationship with the Godhead, through Mary. Praying the Rosary daily, as our Mother asks, is a great way to peace and holiness. With the Rosary, we tell Our Lady and Jesus that we love heaven and hate hell.

Praying the Rosary is asking the Blessed Virgin to help us with our relationship with her Son, Jesus, and to come and do battle for us against the ancient serpent, thereby helping to keep the devil out of our lives. By praying the Rosary, we recognize and employ important scriptural truths from the Book of Genesis through the Book of Revelations. We ask Mary to crush Satan's head, we recognize her as our Mother, and we employ her intercession as Queen of Heaven.

A few people may doubt the efficacy of the Rosary. Some may think it a relic of an earlier spirituality, and others may think it just repetitious nonsense. All of these objections are mere drivel, tools of the devil, meant to keep us away from the graces available to us through the Rosary. The following anecdote is given as an example to help us see the above objections for what they are, nonsense. Our Lady, Virgin Most Powerful loves you.

One Saturday morning James showed to serve Mass. I was the celebrant that morning and had been pastor of the parish for several years. I knew all the servers, yet I had never seen this young man before. He was a tall, handsome teen, a sophomore in high school. Where had he been hiding? Why had I not seen him before? Why hadn't the other priests said something about a new server of such quality? (We always treasured high-school altar servers.) Later I learned the answer to the mystery of his identity and why he showed up to serve that Saturday morning.

James became my best altar server, and after a while he began to open up and share with me the details of how and why he appeared unexpectedly that Saturday morning. By his own admission he had been a typical American teen, which meant that he was rebellious at home and at school, hard to get along with, had a chip on his shoulder, and in general was just an unhappy kid who thought he knew everything.

One evening while flipping channels on television, James per chance ran across The Eternal Word Television Network (EWTN), the popular Catholic channel on TV. There was Mother Angelica saying the Rosary with the sisters of her religious order. James began to pray along with Mother, and surprisingly he began to find peace in his life. He said it was hard to explain, but he began to tune into EWTN every evening when the nuns were praying their community Rosary. Through joining in their Rosaries, James came to understand God's love for him. He recognized that an opportunity to change his life was presenting itself. James developed a great love of the Blessed Virgin and became an outstanding example of what it is to be a disciple of Jesus through Mary. He is now married and has a family of his own. Even today, James will share with you the fact that the Rosary brought him back to the church to stay.

The Virgin Mary has asked us at her apparitions at Fatima to pray the Rosary daily, for the conversion of sinners. She has not changed her mind on this issue. If we want to be obedient children of our Mother, then we need to pray her prayer, the daily Rosary. Our Lady of the Rosary loves you.

Mary is a vital part of our spiritual life just as she, by the grace of God, is an indispensable part of salvation history. She is the perfect disciple of her Son Jesus. Mary is the model of what the church strives to be. Mary is the intercessor par excellence. She is the instrument the Godhead has chosen to throw the beast into hell, and to lock the exits thereof with her Rosary.

The Blessed Virgin Mary is the Queen of Heaven and Earth. She is the Mother of Jesus and by adoption, our Mother. Mary is part of the Father's plan to redeem the human race. Salvation history clearly shows her presence and her role. I pray that her love for us is shown through these pages. I pray that we understand how blessed we are in having Mary as mother, intercessor, model, and more. I hope these words will move people to accept her as Mother and put into practice everything Mother Mary is asking of us. We might get to heaven without a deep devotion to the Virgin Mary, but that would be making things more difficult for us. The easier way, the way the Godhead has planned, is through Mary. Follow the Blessed Mother's example, ask her intercession, and pray her Rosary. We have nothing to lose and all to gain by doing these things. If we follow her then she, the Virgin Mary, will greet us at heaven's door with a beautiful warm smile and lead us to her Son Jesus Christ. Our Lady, Queen of Heaven, loves you.

Road to Priesthood

"You could be a priest!" the voice said. The voice was distinct, clear, and loud enough to catch my attention. It more than perked my interest, it shook me! Who said it? Where did the voice come from? At that moment I was sitting at a table with three other men who were at the other end of the table, engaged in their own conversation, ignoring me completely. I turned to my left and to my right to see who had voiced those definitive and inviting words. There was no one to be seen. There was no one standing behind me. But I had heard those words and they were loud and clear.

No, those words did not come from my imagination. To be a priest was unthinkable! I was not capable of that lofty vocation, and it was a certainty that I was not worthy. With what I had been through in my life I was happy just to be functioning in society. No, those words, "You could be a priest!" did not originate from my faculties, but they were to change my life forever! Years later I came to understand that I had experienced a locution, an inner voice that is not one's own, and that this one was of heavenly origin. It may have been the voice of my guardian angel. It may have been Our Lord himself. I do not know, but I do know my life has not been the same since that moment!

Pondering that amazing statement for a few minutes, I was both excited and at peace. It was true; I was free to become a priest! At thirty-six years old I had no entanglements. I was free to enter the priesthood, if the church would have me, and if I could overcome the mountain of obstacles which stared me in the face, not the least of which would be my speech pattern and my self-confidence, or should I say, the lack thereof.

Allow me to set a few things straight. I had spent the past twenty years of my life expending large amounts of energy avoiding all public speaking. This included even refusing to read a few lines from a newspaper article in front of my own family. How in the world did I ever expect to be able to proclaim the gospel and preach a homily?

Twenty years earlier, at the age of sixteen, I had a whole year's worth of such traumatic experiences that I began to suffer from stuttering. This was in addition to a speech issue that I had already been dealing with, called a lazy speech pattern. (On a lighter note, since I am from the South, many people mistakenly think that this lazy speech pattern is nothing more than a distinctive, if not heavy Southern accent, ya'll.)

Return to the moment when I began to ponder those unbelievable, challenging, and beautiful words: "You could be a priest." I was on a Cursillo weekend, a retreat given by one's peer group for the purpose of changing Sunday-only Catholics into truly active and alive Catholics. Of course there was a priest on board as a spiritual director.

During one of the talks given during the weekend the speaker raised the question, "What could you do to serve God better?" The suggestions thrown out during the talk ranged from becoming a Eucharistic minister, working with the poor, the imprisoned, or the elderly, working with your parish social committee, and everything in between. However, no one suggested a religious vocation. After all, the Cursillo's thrust is for laymen and laywomen, trying to involve them in the nitty-gritty of becoming active members of the parish family.

The talk was over, the stage was set, and I was left with my own thoughts. I deeply desired to turn my life around! I wanted to respond! So I asked myself that question, "What could you do to serve God better?"

"What could I do to serve God better?" The answer hit me like a ton of bricks, "You could be a priest!" Yet it was unthinkable! Me? Thirty-six years old, still not quite settled down, and not having accomplished much in my life up to now, but I gave it some thought anyway. I began to try figure out if it was within the realm of possibilities. There were so many if's in my life still to be dealt with.

Nevertheless, I had to deal with that startling intervention in my life, that locution. I felt an urgency to form a response to those five words, to that challenge. Grace was working. The response that came to me was this: I would not say a word about priesthood to anyone. Rather I would wait to see if I would be selected to be a presenter on a Cursillo team for a weekend such as I was experiencing at that time. If chosen, then I would be able to see how a small group of men would react to me as a speaker, and what my reaction would be to the whole experience of being on a team and of speaking in public. That would give me something to base a decision upon, to judge whether I would be emotionally able to handle being in the public eye.

I felt very safe with the decision because of the manner in which the teams are chosen. Cursillo teams are composed of about twelve men, a majority of whom are team veterans, and the remainder being newcomers. The cushion that I was looking for was this: no one is allowed to be on a team until at least a year after he has made a Cursillo himself. The pool of men from which team members were chosen included anyone from the metro area who had been on a Cursillo in the past. That meant that the pool of those eligible to be a team member would number in the hundreds. The chances of me ever being chosen to be on a team were ever so slight. If Our Lord wanted me to be on a team, he had to defy the odds in a major way. He did!

One year later, almost to the day, I was picked to be on a team! How is that for a push, and a vote of confidence from God! Obviously Our Lord was not interested in the odds or realm of possibilities. He is far above these human ways of viewing things, and they do not influence him in the least. Now I would see whether I had anything of what it takes to be a priest. Now I would see if I could handle the idea of being in the public eye every day. I had run away from public speaking for decades. Now, through God's grace, I had a chance to try to live up to what that voice challenged me to do.

What was the trauma that caused me so much anguish, pain, suffering, anxiety, and guilt? What was it that had ruled my life for two decades and caused my self-confidence to dwindle to almost zero? The answer to these questions will confirm God's never-ending love. In this case the love is showered upon me, but if upon me, then it must be showered upon everyone. He loves all of us! My story will show how everything in our lives can be turned into good. God brings good out of evil. He brings good out of suffering.

I attended a Catholic, all male, non-boarding, military high school. Military schools in the South are an honored tradition. Our culture believes in military training, understanding that it teaches young men many beneficial qualities. It helps build good character, something that stays with you for life.

The school was in the heart of the city, and was run by a religious order of monks. The Catholic girls' school was a block away. Our day started at 8:02 AM with formation, when we spent fifty minutes drilling and performing other military actions. Every now and then the captain of our company would march us down the street right past the girls' school. We all loved it, passing by the girls. We thought we were impressive. The girls from that neighboring school were our main line of communication with the opposite sex. Social functions were well integrated between the two schools.

There were only two Catholic high schools in the city available for boys. The military school was the primary magnet for young men from all over the metro area. To this day the school still enjoys a good reputation for academics as well as sports. It has turned out All-American high school athletes who went on to do the same in college.

On the first day of school my freshmen year, Irritable Bowel Syndrome (IBS) and I had our first appointment. This affliction has remained with me ever since then. Hemorrhages in my nose, upper throat, and mouth become more common for me around this time too. The cause is an inherited disease with the difficult name of Hereditary Hemorrhagic Telangiectasia (HHT). It is estimated that HHT is so rare in the U.S. that there are only five thousand people who have the disease.

I enjoyed the military dimension of school. During my freshman year I achieved a good conduct medal, which was not an easy accomplishment, since the student could not receive more than seven demerits for the whole school year. It was easy to receive demerits. For instance, three demerits were given for having fingerprints on your uniform brass or for talking in class. School was demanding, but I was enjoying life.

Most of my friends from grade school had made the transition to the military school or to the girl's school down the street. Life was exciting and good. Dating and going to the formal dances at school was a blast. Of course we had to double-date with upper classmen that first year, because we could not drive as yet. We would wear our dress whites and the girls would wear dresses with full hoops, very Southern and glamorous for us back in the late 50s. There would be a small orchestra, and it was really something.

In the summers before and after my freshman year of high school, 1958 and 1959, a group of us boys would attend the minor league baseball games in our town. The team was part of the farm system of a major league team. Pay to get into a game? Hardly! If we arrived early enough, the gates were open, and then if we arrived a bit later, there were those holes in the fence that we all knew about.

In the second summer of these light and joyful days, I experienced something that began a difficult period of emotional turmoil in my life. I had no idea what was about to unfold. About seven or eight of us boys were at the game, which was almost over. One of the ushers who was friendly with us asked if anyone needed a ride home. I said yes, even though I usually walked the two miles to my home. Mistake! "Yes" was the wrong answer that night.

The usher was about twenty-six years old, and I was the only one who accepted his invitation. I was a young and naïve fifteen-year-old, and fairly innocent. We got in his car and he began to just drive around rather than taking me home as promised. We drove further and further away from my part of town. Well, to be very straight forward, I was a victim of sexual assault by him. I was scared, nervous, and upset. To this day, I do not fully understand the emotional fright that evening caused within me. Call it rape, call it coerced, and call it horrible!

The moment I opened the front door at home that evening, my parents knew something was wrong. They never put their finger on it, but they knew I had experienced something that had upset me. I kissed them goodnight and went to my bedroom.

I had made up my mind that I was not going to talk about that experience, ever. I wanted to forget it, put it behind me. After all, I had asked for the ride home, and maybe I could have gotten out and ran. Some of the responsibility must be mine; it was my homosexual act, my sin, my disgrace, and my shame. Because of my experience, I understand and sympathize with women and men who suffer from these traumatic, life-changing experiences. It doesn't make sense to many, but blaming oneself for the actions of the predators is common. These creeps, these attackers who prey on the young, know and use this guilty feeling to force their sick perversions on other victims.

Although I went back to the ballpark a few times, I felt as though somebody knew something and that was not good. I did not know what that feeling was all about, but my imagination was not making the best of it. I was never comfortable there anymore, and stopped going to the ballpark. It was my dirty secret. I never discussed it with anyone, never. I did my best to erase that fateful ride home from my memory.

The beginning of my sophomore year saw my life begin to unravel a bit more. I thought I had earned the rank of corporal, but I was passed over. Corporal was a sophomore's rank. Juniors could become sergeants, and seniors held the officer ranks. I never knew why I was passed over, and I never attained a military rank the remainder of my years in high school.

Life took a definitive turn for the worse in the spring semester of my sophomore year. The trauma intensified because of an unwanted sexual approach from a classmate whom I had known most of my life. Individually these things might not have amounted to much, but together they tore me apart, and it would take me decades to recover.

A friend came over to the family home. We had played football together in grade school and he had gone on vacations with my family when we went to the river in the summers. It was a healthy friendship, until that day.

I was privileged to have owned a regulation-sized pool table, so we went down to the recreation room to play. I loved the game of pool then and still do. We played a couple of games and then he approached me sexually. Simply put, I said "No!" We played a few more games of pool, and then drove around town, just goofing off, and that was that. The incident was never spoken of again. However that was not the end of things, although it took a long time for me to put two and two together.

A couple of months later, during lunchtime at school, another longtime schoolmate of mine, with an additional classmate, came up to me and started calling me foul names: G.D. faggot, queer, and the like. They acted in pure hatred, even telling me that I had no right to live. In the background was my friend who had made sexual advances toward me while in my parent's home playing pool. These two bullied and coerced me to step outside of the school building. Then, while one held me, the other beat the hell out of me, while my buddy watched from a distance. I eventually fought them off and defended myself, but real damage had been done, not physically but emotionally, yet again.

I suspect my pool buddy told his peers something to the effect that I was a homosexual. I don't know if this was to take revenge for my non-compliance with his sexual advance, but those other two would never have attacked me without my buddy concocting and spreading lies. Prior to the beating, I was not aware of being on bad terms with anyone in school.

More than fifty years later, I finally remembered that my buddy was part of the group of guys who would hang out at the ballpark. That was the connection! He knew that I had gotten a ride with the usher. Maybe there was something else going on at the ballpark that I didn't know about. Now another dot was connected to make a little more sense of why he had come over my home with the supposed intention of playing pool.

After the thrashing, the in-crowd of my class dropped me. They would act very strange around me, sometimes laugh and walk by or just ignore me completely. This type of behavior has been portrayed well in movies. I began to drift off in two different directions. I withdrew into myself more, and at the same time began to hang out with the kids who were on the fringe, not homosexual, but the slower and/or poorer members of the class, the non-achievers, as some called us. Even though I had some self-respect left and still dreamed dreams of achievement, the parade of traumatic experiences rolled on. During this time, I was dating a super young lady, who was one grade level ahead of me. When she finished high school she became a nun, but she left the religious order when it turned heterodox.

Although I started my junior year with high expectations and a joyful heart, events seemed to conspire to destroy that outlook. The first day of school, our English teacher gave us a book report assignment, to be finished in three weeks. The report was to be on *Gone With the Wind*. I had never read a book anywhere close to its length in my life, but I was up to the task. My report was twenty-six pages long and was done well, except for one major flaw, misspellings. The priest/teacher said if we had more than two misspellings it would result in an automatic "F." Scarlett O'Hara had a double "t" and I only used one "t". The teacher counted each usage of the names as a separate misspelling. I received an "F."

This was not the worst of it. Naively, I told a friend about the frustration I experienced with the grade on the book report and I found out the hard way that he could not be trusted. My friend wrote a humor article for the school newspaper. He announced in his column that I had twenty-five misspellings in my book report with ten pages still to be corrected. I was so embarrassed and humiliated. Some humor!

The day the article came out in the school newspaper was Friday. That night, I had my first automobile accident on the way home from a friend's house. It was not my fault, but what registered with me was the fact that I had an accident. Guiltily, I told myself that I should have been able to avoid it, even though my parents were wonderful about the whole incident.

Three weeks later, when my mother's car had come out of the body shop, I had another accident. Again, it was not my fault. Again, my parents were great. Even so, what was going on? In this instance, I had been in a turning lane, with the blinker turned on when a car plowed into the back of me. The driver had been drinking heavily.

Three weeks after that, another edition of the school newspaper came out and my friend was up to it again. This time he wrote in his column the report card of R_ _ _ _ _ L _ _ _ _ for everyone to see. In a small school, everyone knew whose initials they were. It is true that the report card was the worst I had ever received, but the grades my friend wrote for all to see were a gross exaggeration of my already poor grades. Who would ever think this to be funny? Why would the priest-supervisor of the paper allow such slander? Humiliated! Mortified! Ashamed! Discouraged! Depressed! Yes, I was all of these and more.

I felt as if I had been betrayed by most of my childhood friends. I had had two sexual assaults of which I was ashamed. I was held and beaten by former friends, and laughed at and ridiculed by many in school. My grades were suffering and my parents were in the dark as to why their youngest was not himself. Children, especially teenage boys are capable of being very cruel. Life was dreadful.

At the time the second blurb appeared in the school newspaper, I was attending a class in which the teacher was having everyone read a few paragraphs from the text. He was going up and down the rows of students, having each student read in his turn. When it came time for me to read I began, but for the first time in my life I started to stutter. I got stuck on words like "a" or "the." I actually got so stuck on a word, became so nervous and upset, that nothing would come out of my mouth. I simply stopped reading and put my head down on my desk. I did not know what was happening to me. Life was worse than I could ever explain to anyone. I could not even explain it to myself.

On weekends I would go out with the drinking crowd. We would not get drunk, not very often that is, but would drink quarts of beer and ride around just cruising and exploring city life.

My parents, as I have said before, were wonderful. They did not know what to do for me. They were not aware of what I was going through; at least that is my recollection of things at that time. I was the youngest member of a great Catholic family, and we were all going through a few moments of hell. Just a month into high school, my oldest sister, fifteen years my senior, died of our family disease (HHT). She was only twenty-nine years old, and she left us with two wonderful children. Less than four years later another sister died at the age of twenty-eight. She also left us two beautiful children.

Through all of this tragedy I never heard my parents say a discordant word about God or about the church. I never heard them say anything such as, "Oh! poor me. Why did this have to happen to me?" They were amazing examples of committed Christians, accepting the will of God and moving on in life. My parents carried very heavy crosses. The deaths of their two adult children were just part of their burdens. Now my mother and dad are with their children who went before them into heaven.

Meanwhile, I simply tried to survive. Beginning in the second semester of my junior year, I began to skip a few classes. I fell way behind in math. After taking roll call, the teacher would turn to the blackboard and I would sneak out the door to hang out with some underclassmen, having lunch. Needless to say, I failed that class miserably. I drank a few times at lunch, and then tried to pay attention in the next class. Yeah, right? Life was a mess. I was a mess.

When junior year was over, I had failed three subjects. Until then, I had never failed anything in school. The failures were the crowning to a horrible year. There was something very contrary to all of these failures though. I actually got a "B" in American History that year. We had a new teacher and he was demanding, but I thought his classes were interesting. A majority of the class, including the elite group, failed his class, yet I ended up with that "B." I will not forget the looks on their faces when they realized that the goofball of the class outdid them. They were amazed and befuddled.

I decided that repeating my junior year was better than trying to move forward with the same classmates. If I chose to move ahead with those classmates I would have had to take three summer school classes. That was not a pleasing prospect. I was hoping I would do better with different classmates. It was a good decision and the next semester I began to settle down a bit, doing better socially, and improving academically, too. Even so, the repeating of the grade was discouraging. Not very many students repeat a grade in high school, at least not in my high school. After my fifth year in high school, I was accepted at Belmont Abbey College, a small liberal arts college in North Carolina. I should say that I was accepted on probation because of my difficulties during that one academic year.

I enjoyed college. It was a new beginning, a fresh start. However, being damaged property, I found some aspects of college life to be difficult. My speech problems continued, so I escaped the stress by spending weekends in bars shooting pool. Students were required to take two years of a foreign language and naturally that required reading in class. When it came time for me to read, I tried and tried, but after a semester of stuttering my way through, I found it too emotionally draining, so I would drop the class, not once but three times. Needless to say, I did not finish the college's foreign language requirement, nor did I take any other class in which public speaking was required. That lack of confidence and sense of inferiority stayed with me. What was I to do in real life when I got out into the world? That was my deepest concern.

By the second semester of my sophomore year I at last achieved a "C" average. After finally learning how to study, I came close to making the Dean's List in each semester of the last two years of school. That was a big difference from being accepted on probation, but it was not enough to overcome those fundamental problems that had set me back in high school.

Upon completion of college, I went to work for my dad. He was the proprietor of a small real estate and insurance business. I probably went to work for him because I did not think I could emotionally handle job interviews and was afraid of making a fool of myself with the stuttering. Besides, I had not decided on a path of life. I had been trying to survive. That took most of my energy. It sounds hard to believe for most people, but that was my reality. For me, just surviving was difficult. I do remember once in high school when I mentioned something about priesthood to my mother. Her response was to the effect of, "Well, Robert, you have to be smart to be a priest. You have to learn Latin, you know." That sounded like a final answer to me. I didn't think I could handle languages, so I dismissed that vocation idea from my mind.

The years from the end of college to priesthood saw me travel down an ever-darker road. I was involved in real estate, mostly property management, from the time I was twenty-three until I was almost thirty-eight years old. Those years saw me trying my best to be a good employee for Dad, and at the same time trying to cope with who I was.

I did not like who I was. I bought into the image that my high school friends had molded for me. Two of my sisters died in their late twenties, and I secretly had a desire to join them. Dying would have solved my issues once and for all, but Our Lord had a loving reason for keeping me struggling on in life. Escape was the easy way, but at times it seemed to be the only way.

Those years saw me indulge in a very destructive combination of drugs, alcohol, and a rock 'n' roll life style. I gave up practicing my Catholic faith completely for more than seven years. In my mind I was just trying to survive in a world that I found difficult and depressing. All along I really tried to live by the golden rule, and even though my drugs separated me from my family, I loved them dearly and would visit them often. I was even the favorite uncle to many of my twenty-four nephews and nieces. I was a master of deception, or so I thought. I doubt that my siblings knew that I was living a sub-culture lifestyle until I told them long after those days were over. I did not want them to know because I did not want to cause any harm to them or to give a bad example to their children. I even remember giving a niece an anti-drug talk just before she went away to college. Thirty years later, she still remembered the talk and thanked me for it. Praise God! Our Lord not only kept me alive, no easy task during those years, but also preserved my mind pretty much intact. He is so merciful and patient with all of his people.

In March of 1977, as I was nearing my thirty-third birthday, my life was empty, a desert. I was desperately trying to hold onto life itself, and one day I found myself in the back of the church my parents helped to build in 1928 and in which I had grown up. It is a beautiful Romanesque brick church, which survived the spirit of Vatican II and remains beautifully intact. It was a weekday and no one else was there except Jesus, of course. I had thrown away the gift of my faith, but I sat in the last pew and tried to find a bit of sanity in the quiet of this fine-looking edifice known as Saint Benedict Catholic Church. Although I was inspired to remember that what happens on the altar is our covenant with God, I could not make a connection between the altar, the covenant, and me. I could almost see a physical barrier or chasm between the sanctuary and me, and I was reminded of the story in the Bible of Lazarus and the rich man who had both died. Here I was with the rich man on one side of the great divide and Jesus and Lazarus were on the other, with no way for me to reach Jesus, salvation, or heaven, which are all part of the same goal.

As I sat, I began praying for the gift of faith, recognizing that in my attempt to escape life I had wasted that precious gift. I recall the day as if it were only a moment ago. I had never been needier, never more hurting, never in more pain, and never more desperate. As always, God heard my prayers! With and through God's grace I made up my mind that I would indeed come back to church, with all that it entailed. I would do my best to live the faith, and to be faithful to the magisterium and to all of her teachings. My good Catholic education was finally paying off. I remembered!

I had been trying to live as the world teaches, to live for today, and that brought me no happiness, only deeper despair and emptiness. The world had nothing to offer. Everything worldly is relative, with nothing solid to base life on. It offers no rules, no morals, and no true love, just a hedonistic here-and-now lifestyle that goes nowhere fast and is always unfulfilling.

Contrary to the world, the Catholic church offers the faith of the apostles on which to plant our feet. She is the "one, holy, catholic, and apostolic church," the church which Christ founded upon the Rock, Saint Peter. The church understands and teaches that there is such a thing as eternal truth, and that truth does not change with each individual or with the age in which we live. Truth is truth; if it was truth in Jesus' time, it is truth today. Jesus is the truth! The church lost almost the entire British Isles because she, the church, would not bend to the powers of the day nor to the understanding that truth can be circumvented, changed, or ignored. The church is the Rock.

I was on the right road! God was working within me and I was beginning to listen. Within two weeks of that date, I made a sacramental confession. I was so nervous that I downed a couple of beers before going into the box. It had been more than seven years since I made a good confession. The confessional was an old-fashioned one where the priest sits between two kneelers, with just a heavy cloth to cloak him from the rest of church, and a small screen between the penitent and confessor. As I left the confessional, I glanced back and noticed that the priest had pulled the cloth aside to see who had just confessed. God bless him! I probably made his hair curl!

Once I had received the sacrament of Penance, I began to go to Mass several times a week. I was rusty, but I knew I was home and that I needed to be there. The church was the only thing that made sense in life. A few years later my mother told me that she and dad had been praying every day for me in two ways. First, they prayed to the Blessed Virgin Mary to keep me safe during my wanderings. Secondly, they prayed to her spouse, the Holy Spirit, for him to give me the gift of faith.

How about that! Isn't that what I asked of the Holy Spirit when I sat in the back of Saint Benedict Church? It seemed that my parents had been praying for the same thing for me for years. I am sure it was their prayers which led me to seek faith myself. God does not force himself on anyone. He wants to be invited, and I did that with my own prayer request for faith. My petition was the door that Jesus needed to be opened so that he could light the fire of love in my heart. My parents were the ones who had been asking for that year after year.

The alcohol and marijuana use did not stop cold-turkey when I returned to church. From that fateful day in March 1977, I quit socializing with the sub-culture type of people and I did lighten up on both alcohol and pot, but their use had been ingrained in my life. I recognized that it was a conflict, but I truly was working on it. Over the next three years, I did make some progress in life. I gave up a bad three-pack-a-day cigarette habit, and achieved some success in real estate. I became a real-estate broker, and earned a specialized designation for property management, which came in handy later when I became a pastor.

Nevertheless, in February of 1980, I was facing another crisis in my life. I was in real danger of being picked up for possession of illegal substances. So I dropped to my knees and told Our Lord that if he got me out of a particular situation, I would go cold turkey on the illicit drugs. He did. And I did. From February until the middle of June, I did not have anything illicit. Then I had a particularly bad week at work, succumbed and began smoking a little pot in the evenings just to keep the edge off. I was not happy with this, but I thought this was the best I could do. I thought God understood, and of course he did, although that is not the same as his approval.

Let's return to that Cursillo of October 1980. Sometime on that weekend, before the locution, which offered me an opportunity and a challenge, I was infused with a certain knowledge of the everlasting, faithful, and infinite love that God had for me. He made me understand that all of those years of trying to escape, and my participation in a sub-culture life, did not matter to him. What did matter to Our Lord was my response to his love at that present moment. He wanted me to understand that his love is unconditional and unchanging.

I must have gone through a visible transformation on my Cursillo weekend. My sister-in-law, who attended the closing Mass and ceremonies, went home and told my brother and their children that I was going to be a priest. They laughed her out of the room, thinking that she was nuts. I had not said a word about priesthood to anyone, and would not do so for fifteen more months. Twenty-four hours later, I ran into one of my brothers-in-law. Without even saying hello, he proclaimed, "I am going on Cursillo. I want what you have!" Obviously Our Lord touched me with a deeply-felt knowledge of his love. I knew it on the inside and everyone else could see it manifested on the outside.

All of those years of doubting myself, of having no confidence, of thinking I could never accomplish anything, of feeling worthless, and of being less than I should have been, were all erased because of one weekend when God reached down and touched me so deeply that I kept a joyful smile on my face for two years.

During the year after my Cursillo, I joined two group reunions of men who had been on Cursillo; both groups met once a week. I joined the Elderly and Shut-in Committee at the parish. I became a Eucharistic minister, and was on the parish Social Committee. I also kept a paroled prisoner in my home for a few months. He had been in prison for seventeen years; his offence was that of murdering a pimp in some country bar.

Not least of the miracles from my Cursillo weekend was that I have never touched an illicit substance since! Our Lord is totally responsible for the transformation in me. He touched me and erased much of the garbage that I had been accustomed to carrying around. I have had my share of his cross to bear since then, but that one weekend was sufficient to change my life forever!

Now I had to see if I had what it took to be in the public eye for the rest of my life. I had been selected to be on a Cursillo team, one year almost to the day after I had been a candidate myself. During formation for the team, we met weekly for almost three months, working on talks, trying to grow together as a unit, and planning details of the weekend. During one of these meetings, I was asked to read a short article to the group. I would not be understating or stretching the facts to say that I did a miserable job trying to read that piece. In fact, up until then I had been scheduled to do a reading at a Mass on the weekend. However, after reading that article, the assignment simply evaporated.

My talk was to be presented on Sunday afternoon, the third day of the Cursillo. The complication to me was that I had three days extra to become even more nervous. Then the time came to give my talk, my first public speaking in more than twenty years. I remember racing through the prepared talk so I would not stutter. The problem was that I spoke so fast that few if any understood what I was speaking about. Whew! I did give a horrible talk but I was enormously relieved to have it behind me.

The Christian witness, which I delivered much more slowly than the prepared talk, was strong. My witness followed immediately after that incoherent talk. I spoke about the drugs, the sub-culture life-style, and how my life changed for the better during my own Cursillo weekend, a year earlier. I spoke about my new involvement in church activities and group reunions that were one result of the many graces I received on that Cursillo weekend. While my assigned talk was awful, my recounting of the 180 degree turn-around in my life was an enormous success! It sold many on the efficacy of the Cursillo methodology.

Afterwards I went and sat next to the spiritual director. It was obvious that I was looking for affirmation. He looked at me and said, "Effective." That was all he said, but that was what I needed to hear. It took a while to sink in, but I began to recognize that, if I had any gift, it was that my sincerity came through in my witness; I naturally speak from my heart.

What was a table leader? I was one on Cursillo. All candidates were assigned a particular table for the entire weekend. The table leader was a team member whose main duty was to be a facilitator. He would keep the discussion going, keep interest up, answer questions, and be a cheerleader for the candidates.

Just before the closing Mass on Sunday, the candidates were invited to stand and share their thoughts, if they wished, with everyone present for the Mass and closing ceremonies. Well, this older man who was at my table stood up and began to speak very highly of a team member. He went on and on, even calling this person a ringer. At the end of all of this he pointed to me and named me as being the ringer. The whole congregation stood and gave me a round of applause. I was floored!

A year earlier, I had told the Lord that I would consider priesthood if I could be on a Cursillo team to see how the candidates and team reacted to me, and how I reacted to them. One year later I was on a team. I lived through the talk, and that is the best I can say about that. However, at the closing Mass I received that standing ovation, true affirmation that something positive was taking place in my life. Somehow I must have been on the right track. The stuttering was still very much an issue but I felt that I must press forward. God opened the door to be on a Cursillo team. If he wanted me to be a priest, he must continue to open those doors.

What was the next step? The spiritual director for the Cursillo suggested that I go on a silent retreat to discern the call to priesthood. With the words of the locution, "You could be a priest," clearly in head and heart, I felt no need for the retreat, but I was obedient and complied. The retreat took place in January of 1982. It was an unusually cold January. Even the rivers in Virginia were frozen over, a rarity indeed.

Having never been on a retreat, much less one that required silence, I enjoyed the unique experience. I had conferences with the priest who was our spiritual director several times a day, did my assigned homework, studied and reflected on special scripture passages. I also took long walks along the railroad tracks that ran parallel to a river down the hill from the retreat center. It was so wonderful to consider the possibilities of a new life closer to Our Lord. Recognizing his love spurred me on to try anything that I thought would please him. Now I identify this drive, this overwhelming enthusiasm, as first fervor, a very necessary ingredient if I were to push on in seeking ordination to priesthood.

Coming home after the retreat was one of the most joyful moments of my life. At that time I was living with my parents. However, I had not told them why I was on the retreat. Mother, Dad, and I sat down in the dining room at home so I could speak with them. When I revealed that I was applying to the diocese to study for priesthood, the moment was indescribable! My parents had watched me throw away my faith and live a destructive lifestyle. Now I was saying that I was to try to study for priesthood. Pen and paper could not ever describe such a moment! All three of us sat around the table and cried a bit, and then a bit more. The older I become, the more I understand the deep love and concern they both had for me.

Even so, I still had to be accepted by a diocese and admitted to a seminary. I had a bachelor's degree, but did not know how much education would be required of me in the seminary before ordination. Who would pay for the education? Would I be able to see family very often? What would life be like in the seminary? What were priests like? Now that was a comical question! I had always tried to stay away from priests, and now I was going to study to be one? God is so funny.

I was accepted by two dioceses and with the guidance of a priest friend I decided to study for the Diocese of Arlington Virginia. I was sent to Mount Saint Mary's Seminary in Emmitsburg, Maryland. I reported to the seminary in August of 1982. It had been twenty-two months since I had first heard the definitive call to priesthood. I was thirty-eight years old and was beginning a new life. That first night in the seminary with a hundred and eighty other men who were in love with Jesus was intoxicating. I hardly slept.

Seminary offered some interesting adjustments. Sharing a bathroom with forty men was a real shocker. The bathroom was large, but having had my own space for years and now walking into something like that was not the most pleasant way to start a day! Having a roommate for the first year and a half was an adjustment too, but bathrooms and roommates aside, the seminary was a good experience, especially the classes and prayer life.

Of immediate concern to me was how soon I would have to speak in public. I knew that it was inevitable and that once it began, it would be constant. I was pleased to hear that second year theologians took the Office of Reader around Thanksgiving. That meant no public speaking, as far as I knew, until then. I had a year-and-a-half to work on overcoming my speech issues.

Let me say a few words about the Office of Reader. The new readers were assigned as reader for the day, meaning that they would not only read at Mass, but also during the communal recitation of morning and evening prayers. The seminary assigned readers alphabetically. Praise God! That meant that I would not read in public until after the Christmas break.

Things were reaching what I considered to be a critical moment, so over the Christmas break I went on a weeklong silent retreat with a group of hermits in New Jersey. Everyone on the retreat had his own small hermitage. We came together only for prayers and meals, which were in silence as well. Wednesdays at the hermitage were days of strict fasting, meaning bread and water only. My reason for going that extra mile, to attend a retreat which was not required, was to petition Our Lord for help regarding my speech issues. I wanted him to take away or lighten up my speech difficulties, so I could function as the priest I knew he wanted me to become. What was I to do if I continued to stutter and stammer in front of my peer group? What would the administration do to me? Seven days of silence, prayer, and fasting was difficult but most stimulating, as Our Lord would have it.

After all that time spent in fasting and prayerful solitude, I came away from the retreat with the understanding that Our Lord was saying to me, "My grace is sufficient for you." He did not take away the problem, but promised to be with me as I continued my struggle. The fasting made me a bit thinner too.

Back at the seminary, on February 2, the Feast of the Presentation of the Lord, an unforgettable experience occurred. That was my first day to be a reader in the seminary. Because it was a feast day, I would have not one reading, but two, with a sung responsorial hymn between the two readings. Feast days also meant that every priest on the faculty would be concelebrating. More readings and more priests meant more pressure. I was a nervous wreck! The moment finally arrived to do my readings. I had been anticipating this moment of truth since that definitive call to priesthood, three-and-a-half years earlier.

It was almost comical. I read very quickly (sound familiar?) so that I would not stutter and stammer. When it came time for the homilist to speak, he had to paraphrase my readings in order for the congregation to understand what it was he was speaking about. However I did live through it, and no one in the administration said a negative word to me. Alleluia!

That one experience as a lector was all the public speaking required of me that semester, but at the end of that school year, I was assigned to work in a parish, my first parish assignment. I was to live in a rectory for ten weeks. One of my most important tasks that summer would be to do the first reading at all the Masses—ten weeks' worth. A piece of cake for most seminarians, but for someone who had lived with a fear of reading in public for over twenty years, it was a different story. I was determined to face the issue head on, but I was not looking forward to it at all.

Although I practiced every day, standing at the podium and reading aloud, I was awful. It happened that the cycle of readings included endless lists of difficult Old Testament names. After a week or so of enduring these attempts, my pastor had compassion for me (or was it for his congregation?). No matter, he began to help me read. He slowed me down and helped me to enunciate. By the end of the summer, I was doing better. Life did not seem as hard to conquer as it had before. I thought I could see light down the road.

As I entered the third year of theology, my ordination to priesthood was getting closer, I hoped. At the end of that school year, God willing, I was to be ordained a deacon, and then it would be just one more year to priesthood. The first semester went well, but things were going to change just after the Christmas break. Some serious testing was to come.

In those days I was a jogger, running three to five miles a day, until exam week of the first semester. Then unexpectedly, the HHT bleeding disorder acted up. I had my first debilitating nose bleed and I went home for Christmas tired, not realizing that I was suffering from anemia. Returning to the seminary in early January, I promptly caught the flu. The anemia enabled the flu to take a strong hold and made it hard to shake. I had no defense. I was sick, really sick.

During a scripture class on the Gospel of John, the priest/professor told us students to open our Bibles and follow along as he read. Being tired and sick, I was trying to listen intently rather than pick up my Bible from under my desk, an effort for me that day, due to the flu and anemia. Besides I didn't think it was that big deal of an issue.

The priest did not like being disobeyed, so he ordered me to read a passage to the class. Immediately, I had flashbacks to all those horrible days of high school. Instantly I became my old self. It didn't help matters that I was tired, anemic and sick from the flu. I did a lousy job in reading. Was I back to square one?

Two weeks later, the rector of the seminary came to my room with a serious look on his face. He informed me, as gently as he could, that he had been notified that I could not read. He said that if I could not read I could not be ordained a deacon. My diaconate ordination was just four months away! I was floored by this new hurdle.

I had given up my day job, my career, such as it was, and given two-and-a-half years of my life to study for priesthood. Now I might not be ordained? I had vowed to Our Lord back in October of 1980 that I would persevere in trying to become a priest until he either told me no, or followed through with making me the priest that I thought he wanted me to be.

I went to the rector's office where he asked me to read a few lines from some text. I was nervous and upset; were these excuses or were they reasons? I did my usual bad job of reading. Have I mentioned that the rector was a great person? He was! He put me in contact with a couple of English professors in the college, and asked that they work with me so I could get over this block and finally learn to read.

And they did, thank God! It was embarrassing, humiliating, and hard work for me, but totally worth every anxious moment and bead of sweat that I experienced. I learned to read aloud at forty years old. I learned to read for the first time since I was sixteen. It might not seem like much to most people, but for me that was some hurdle! It was evidence that God's grace was working. (Thinking back, I now recognize that this hurdle was a gift from God to settle this reading issue, once and for all.)

My problem with speech was not over, but it was cleared up sufficiently enough for me to be ordained. God was true to his promise! His grace was sufficient. He did not take away the problem, but he gave me the courage and strength to work through it. That struggle made me a better person. For years into priesthood I would have to practice reading from the Lectionary ahead of time.

So that was part of my long and painful struggle to overcome stuttering. Through it all I have recognized that I have nothing to boast of myself. As Saint Paul rightfully proclaimed the he "could boast only in the cross of Our

Lord." God chooses the lowly and weak of the world and makes them something. I believe this is true for two reasons. First, he does it to illustrate his own humility, and secondly to confound the proud and arrogant.

How about my singing? Well, people continue today to chide me because of my lack of ability to sing. The only part I try to sing at Mass is "Through him, and with him, and in him . . ." Every time I raise the precious Body and Blood of Our Savior and sing, I return to him what he has given me, and if it leads to a little embarrassment on my part and some penance on the part of the congregation, well, so be it!

What about my homilies? No one would ever say that I am a great speaker. I am not eloquent and surely not intellectual. However, my homilies do come across as being most sincere and serious. I am ever so grateful for God's unfailing love for me. Our humble God is so patient. I am able to speak from the heart about everything pertaining to salvation and our wonderful loving God. My sermons are meat-and-potato style: simple, catechetical, and sacramentally based. This is the way God has gifted his people through my preaching.

What a long road that was! From refusing to read a sentence from a newspaper article in my parents' home, I have moved to speaking in front of large congregations every Sunday. Only God could effect that change in a person.

The priest who knew me best in pre-seminary days was a good man. At a dinner in my home I asked him directly, "Father, what kind of education is required to become a priest?" He asked, "For whom?" and I replied, "For me." Saying nothing, he simply turned his head and continued to speak with my other guest. Thus he answered with his silence, implying that I had no vocation. He did not think I had what it took to be a priest. He had known me since grade school, but dismissed my ability to become a priest by not answering the question I asked him. This incident took place between the time of my first Cursillo, and when I joined the Cursillo team. It was January of 1981.

I became a diocesan priest rather than a religious order priest because of the answer from my priest-friend. However, all things work towards God's plan. Our Lord wanted me in a parish setting, so he allowed the attitude of that priest to discourage me from joining a religious order. As things turned out, it is obvious to me now that I am not well suited to be in a religious order.

God knows best. He knew that my brokenness would actually help to make me the priest that I am. He used all my years of suffering and escape to better assist other wayward Christians who need an understanding ear, someone who has experienced the darker side of life, someone who has time for them. Those of us who have received a special infusion of knowledge regarding Our Lord's personal love for us seem to be able to reach the lonely, those on the fringes, those who deal with depression, and those who have no hope. For some reason, my homilies hit home with these people who are the more broken among us. I am so blessed. Who would have ever thought?

Priesthood is the treasure of my life!

You Are A Priest Forever

You are a priest forever according to the order of Melchizedek (Ps. 110:4).

It all came true. God's grace reigned! I was ordained by the hands of Bishop John Richard Keating, Bishop of Arlington in the Cathedral of Saint Thomas More, on May 10, 1986. I was by far the oldest in my ordination class of five and maybe the most grateful, as it took me forty-one years, ten months, and twenty-seven days to become the priest that Our Lord wanted me to be from day one.

Praise God that there were other men being ordained that day, making life a bit more comfortable. It was indeed wonderful and exciting! Ordination was the finale of years of formation and study. It was the culmination of years of prayer from a grateful mother. It was the beginning of a life that always seemed out of reach for one so broken as I.

My first Mass was celebrated in the parish church my parents helped to build in 1928. Saint Benedict Church has been home to my family since before the cornerstone of that classic Romanesque structure was laid. It is a historical church in our family for many reasons, and the very smell of the church reminds me of home. The first Mass of mine was a sacred covenant being celebrated, yes, but it was also a gathering of a grateful community praising God for the good work done in a new priest. There were about three hundred people who attended the late Sunday afternoon Mass. Many were from families that I have known my entire life. Most of them knew of my struggles, and they were present that day for a victory celebration of God's healing and transforming love in me.

On both sacramental and personal levels, I cannot express the height of emotional and spiritual joy, experienced and expressed in Saint Benedict Church, in Richmond, Virginia, that warm May afternoon. Those few minutes lived in history only once, but the depth of multifaceted joy of those moments returns to my consciousness when I recall that most special celebration of my life. Possibly I have experienced more sacred moments, however this was a combination of many other factors, too many to even recount.

How appropriate that I celebrated my first Mass on Mother's Day! This struggling soul who was dedicated to the Virgin Mary at Baptism and who returned to the church because of a mother's prayers, celebrated his first Mass on a day that made it easy and natural to honor both his biological mother and Mother Mary, with the gift of Jesus, her son. After Holy Communion, I received a rose from my mom and placed it on Mary's altar as a way of saying, "Mary, I hereby dedicate my share in the priesthood of your son, Jesus Christ, to you."

My family provided me with an elaborate celebration after the first Mass. Again, it was a celebration of God's love. All three hundred came to the reception. I was so involved with the celebration of the moment that I did not have the chance to even taste the delicious foods that were served. All of this was the conclusion of years of prayer and study, of worry and anxiety. The reality was setting in, "You are a priest forever" . . . I would have about a month of vacation time before I had to settle down and begin the work which I would come to love. As time went by, I would come to understand that I was most gifted by Christ choosing me to become his priest.

The day after my first Mass a friend and I drove to the beach for a few days. That first evening he asked if I would hear his confession. The words stunned me! I was a priest, and my privilege was to reconcile man to God. Reality set in! My first confession was to be from a very close friend. I was so wet behind the ears that I had to find my rites book so I could read the absolution, not having memorized it yet.

In three days, from Saturday to Monday, I was ordained, celebrated Mass, and heard my first confession. I didn't realize it at the time, but those two sacraments, Eucharist and Penance, were to become my very life, as they are the lifeblood of the church which keep us all on the narrow road to heaven.

Exactly six years later, my first penitent offered his first Mass. I was privileged to deliver the homily at his Mass. I began by thanking God for his belated vocation, but then I shared with the congregation about my first penitent being the new priest now celebrating his first Mass. I related how in Canon Law, there is a special canon whereby the seal of confession does not apply to your first penitent. (Of course that is not true, but the congregation loved it.) The celebrant's face turned purple. That was fun!

It is said that if a priest truly understood the depths of his actions while saying Mass, he would be unable to actually do so. The magnificence of God's love being showered upon his people through the Mass is overwhelming. Every time a priest says Mass, the paschal mystery is re-presented in our time. What happened two thousand years ago is truly made present again. It is not a new crucifixion of Christ.

It is the trans-historical event which took place on Calvary with Mary Magdalene, John the Beloved, and the Blessed Mother all present at the foot of Jesus' cross. That is the event that is made present to us every time a priest says Mass.

People ask me how it feels to be a priest and celebrate Mass. Can a priest accurately give a sufficient answer to spiritual realities that cannot be put into words? How does anyone express his intellectual, spiritual, and emotional thoughts and feelings when involved intimately in the act which brings salvation to the world?

Intellectually, I have always understood the essential nature of the Mass and the function of the priest, the one who offers the sacrifice. However, in the beginning of my priesthood, there was a consuming consciousness of trying to say Mass without making a big blunder. The attention to details was of great concern at first, and maybe even of supreme importance for a while, for a couple of reasons: my own pride and not wanting to distract the congregation from their prayerful participation.

Over time the rubrics fell into place and I became more comfortable thereby enabling myself to pay attention to the overwhelming spiritual actions in which I was participating. Additionally, I learned that if I don't prepare for Mass by having time in prayer before the Blessed Sacrament or at least have a few minutes of meditation in my room before going into the sacristy, then I have a good chance of becoming only a functionary for that Mass. I go through the actions of saying Mass, but there is no heartfelt response from within me, nothing spiritual. It all escapes.

Saint Charles Borromeo reminded the priests of his day that what I have learned is true. The quality of one's participation in Mass depends upon his actions before Mass. Saint Charles would ask, "How well did you prepare?" We read this passage every year from the *Liturgy of the Hours* on his feast day and how true it is, how true it is.

A modern sacristy is no place to prepare to say Mass. People stop by to leave this and that for other priests or they return vestments, altar boys are goofing around, lectors arrive, and well-meaning visitors come by, all making for busyness before Mass. If a priest says something about needing quiet, he is labeled as a grouch and people stay away from him, and they talk behind his back. It's a frustrating situation. To pray in church or in your room is the way to properly prepare to celebrate the sacred mysteries.

As the years have progressed and the number of Masses celebrated has accumulated, I pronounce the same words at Mass, but, Oh, how I have come to treasure the pure gift of celebrating the covenant between God and his people! Although I am not required to say Mass daily, it takes quite a lot to keep me from the altar. I imagine that over the last twenty-six years of priesthood, I have missed offering Mass only about thirty days during the years of my priesthood.

If the priest prepares properly, the magnitude of the sacrament is overwhelming! How is the priest truly able to understand and appreciate his role in this mystical gift of love from the infinite God to his sinful and finite children? At his words, Jesus becomes present to us. God obeys man? Yes! Even if the priest is in mortal sin! How humble. How loving. How merciful. And how needed!

It is through the paschal mystery that we enter into the new and eternal covenant with God our Father. It is through the blood of Christ poured out for us that the covenant is sealed. This is what we celebrate every time a priest says Mass. When the priest utters the words of consecration, the words of Jesus himself at the Last Supper, it is the priest's voice, but it is Christ speaking through the priest. The Last Supper is made present to us once again. We participate in the Last Supper as if we were truly there when Jesus instituted the Eucharist and priesthood.

I am totally humbled by being a priest of Jesus Christ and absolutely awed by it too! There are so many facets, and so much depth to each facet that it overpowers the mind. "For God so loved the world as to give his only-begotten Son, that whosoever believeth in him may not perish but have life everlasting" (Jn. 3:16). The priest is the instrument who makes the mystery of Christ's sacrifice on the cross present to his people of every generation, each day until his second coming.

My first official confession scheduled was a mere six days into active ministry. The faith and trust of the parishioners were awe-inspiring that first day. I was so thrilled and happy to be part of the healing process for these ordinary people. To absolve someone became my second favorite activity and duty as a priest. Any priest soon becomes familiar with the many different styles of making one's confession. Some penitents are very shy and afraid, others are sort of bold and loud, still others are truly troubled and need a priest's compassionate heart and a little spiritual direction too. Certain penitents, because of nervousness or some other reason, even tell the priest how good they have been! No matter who the penitent is, pronouncing the words of absolution soon becomes extremely satisfying to the priest, even more so as the years pass.

Most of us do not enjoy going to confession. I do not enjoy going either, but I go regularly. I think part of my job is to make confessing sins easier for the penitents. I never try to minimize the sinfulness of what they have done, but help to bring them the forgiveness they seek, as if Christ were saying the words himself to encourage, correct, and forgive. I see the priest as reconciling, as well as being a vehicle of hope for sinners. After all, priests need a redeemer too. There is no such thing as an ordinary confession.

All confessions are special. All involve bringing a soul closer to Christ. I often preach on the necessity of regular confession. Frequenting the sacrament at least once a month is a positive step in making one's way to heaven.

Confession is an act of humility, the opposite of the worst of all sins, pride. That is why many people find it difficult to approach the sacrament. If we would realize that humility is the gateway to a positive relationship with God, we might find the courage to overcome our pride. Many of the great saints tell us that without humility, there can be no positive relationship with God. Humility opens the door to God's love and forgiveness. Asked what were the three greatest virtues, Saint John Vianney replied, "humility, humility and humility."

When we act in humility we act as God does. Our God is humble. He is perfect humility. Why else would he have become a man and redeemed mankind? The Incarnation is an act of humility beyond our comprehension! He gave us examples of humility when he was born as a man … "one tempted in all things like as we are, without sin," (Heb. 4:15), as in when he washed the feet of the apostles, and when he suffered and died on the cross. The gospels abound with similar examples.

When you go to confession, you make all of heaven smile! Why? Because you have opened the door to God's healing presence, his love. Not only that, but you move Jesus very deeply. You touch his heart, because you tell him, by your actions, by going to confession, that you take seriously his salvific action on the cross.

Please always be aware of this reality and never fear the sacrament of Penance. Rather, view it as the God-given vehicle by which we are forgiven our transgressions, and are drawn closer to Our Lord and to our heavenly reward, the eternal banquet. This fear is not from God but rather is a tactic employed by the beast who lives below to keep us from achieving our eternal happiness. God wants to bring us joy and peace, while the beast brings fear, anxiety, depression, anger, and negativity.

We also need to know that when we go to confession, God always forgives our sins and showers us with the grace to do better. Of course, we must confess all mortal sins, have sorrow for offending our God, and have a firm purpose of amending our lives.

God's mercy flows from the Holy Sacrifice of the Mass directly into the confessional. While all confessions are a joy, others are more powerfully felt because of the nature of the sin confessed, the sincere sorrow of the penitent, or because of the deep conversion that takes place before the eyes of the priest. While the following examples may seem exceedingly unusual, they are also ordinary due to the fact that they are available to all people at all time, and that they take place somewhere in the world every day.

The accounts which follow have been sufficiently altered so that there is no chance of identifying an actual penitent. If you respond to Christ's love by approaching him in confession, no matter what condition your soul may be in, you will have a positive experience as well as being a good influence on others.

One case in point concerns a lady who came to the sacrament of Confession after being away for twenty-five years. Because Our Lord pursued her and did not give up on her, many wonderful things happened and are still happening in her life and in the lives of others.

After my normal weekday Mass, I walked from the sacristy through the nave of the church and on to the confessionals. Passing by a lady who had a most apprehensive look on her face, my glance told me that she was deeply distraught. She was distressed because the devil was trying to keep her from confessing her sins, while confession actually was the solution to her problems. However, she did make her confession that afternoon and was absolved of twenty-five years of sins. As always happens in a confession like that, she even sounded like a different person after the absolution was administered. Because she re-embraced her faith, her child was brought into the church. He had never been baptized. Now that boy is a young Catholic man who practices the faith that Christ has given him.

This same penitent had her marriage blessed in the church! The good news continued. One of her in-laws was so influenced by her that the relative made a sacramental confession, the first in almost a half-century! The in-law was back in the church for good, thanks to that one lady who came to her senses and reconciled with the church through the sacrament of Penance. The effects of her coming back to her faith continue to ripple across the waters of life in many positive ways.

A woman had a terminal disease and was in denial of her sinfulness. That is not a good position to take. At the request of one of her old friends, I went to the hospital to try to intercede on behalf of Christ. She was aware of her terminal illness, but told me she had led a good life, trying to give the impression that there was nothing to fear. As the conversation continued, I was able to show her where the sins were, and reminded her that she was responsible for them before her eternal judge.

The good news is that I did hear her first confession in close to six decades. When I left her hospital room that evening, after giving her absolution and also the Anointing of the Sick, she looked years younger. Her smile was from ear to ear. That is one of the great joys of priesthood. I will never forget her peaceful, joyful smile.

The next weekend she attended Mass and as she approached the altar to receive Holy Communion, I could see tears streaming down her cheeks. Her tears were of joy, because after almost six decades, she was able to receive Christ her Lord in the Eucharist. After Mass she gave me a big hug and thanked me profusely. Her joy was tangible. I will not forget that, either. Of course all credit goes to almighty God for his infinite love and for the patience that he has shown to each of us.

The woman died just weeks later, but before that face-to-face meeting with Our Lord, she had reconciled with him and his church. God is so gracious! She was snatched from the fires of hell and raised up to the consuming fire of God's infinite love.

A few days after Easter an old man walked into my office and inquired if I had time for a confession. "Yes, of course," was my immediate reply. As he sat down he began without hesitation saying, "Bless me, Father, for I have sinned. It has been seventy-three years since my last confession." Shivers of joy went down my spine. He was my biggest fish ever! I was so happy he was confessing; there is no way he could know how pleased I was to be God's instrument to save him from the fires of hell and place him firmly into the arms of his loving Savior. To say that he made my day would have been the gross understatement of the year. his confession was pure consolation.

The big fish had led a wildly secular life, but God gave him the grace to return to the sacraments. Big Fish even knew the Act of Contrition perfectly. He walked into the office as if he were dragging, but he left smiling and hardly touching the floor, and when he attended Mass on Sunday, he came down the aisle to receive his Lord crying just like our lady friend who had been away from church for almost six decades. In fact, I have been privileged to witness that same joy in peoples' hearts numerous times. This is a gift of priesthood which I cannot readily share with others. I am always moved deeply by God's infinite patience and mercy.

I cannot say it often enough or loud enough; God's love for each of us is endless! It is constant; its depth is bottomless, and it is centered on our salvation.

The parish office was a walk-through from the priests' parking area to the rectory living quarters. Returning from a dinner engagement, I was on the way to the bathroom and just happened at that moment to be passing through the closed office. I answered the phone to find out that the father-in-law of a good friend, a doctor by trade, was being transported to the hospital because he was having a heart attack.

Timing was everything. If the phone had rung a minute earlier or a minute later, no one would have been there to answer. A minute earlier and I would still be driving back to the rectory. A minute later and I would have been in the restroom. This was before our rectory had answering services or office boys in the evening. The parishioners were often on their own if no priest happened to be in to answer the phone.

I was asked to meet the ambulance at the hospital to see what I could do for the doctor who was having the heart attack. I was told that the patient might not welcome me because he had not practiced his faith for over forty years.

As I made my through the emergency room, I found the doctor-patient in a cubicle. He was lying on a gurney with not much on other than a green scapular, which I thought unexpectedly strange. An attending physician and others were around, so I found it impossible to say anything privately to the patient, thus making a detailed confession unworkable. He looked up at me and said something such as, "You're a little late for me, Father." I said, "Not true! All God wants to know is if you are sorry for your sins." He answered, "Yes!," so I absolved him. He died three hours later.

Some incredible things need to be pointed out. I was there to answer the phone in the rectory. Coincidence? Hardly! The doctor-patient had led a good Catholic life from childhood into college, even was active in the Newman Society in college. Yet, just after that he turned into a strong opponent of the church.

His son-in-law, my friend, had shown the doctor a video about the apparitions at Fatima, with Ricardo Montalban as the narrator. It is an excellent documentary, giving an accurate account of the Blessed Mother's apparitions in Portugal in 1917. After watching the whole presentation, the doctor turned to his son-in-law and said, "That was the greatest piece of Catholic propaganda I have ever seen." He was a hard case indeed.

My friend had offered the doctor the brown and the green scapulars a number of times. Always the doctor would refuse and make fun of the spirituality of his son-in law. This went on for years. Yet for some reason (God's will?) the man put on the scapular a week before he had the heart attack.

After hearing his confession, (It had to be in general terms because of the lack of privacy), I visited with his daughters, who told me that their dad was supposed to recover and be home in a few days. God knew better, because within three hours it was all over. The doctor had met his eternal judge. That meeting went well because he had expressed sorrow for his sins and had been forgiven through the sacrament of Penance just before that mandatory meeting. God's love is persistent and unchanging.

The sacrament of the Anointing of the Sick, also referred to as Extreme Unction, is the most misunderstood of the seven sacraments. Most Catholics are not aware that this great sacrament includes the forgiveness of sins. (If the recipient is physically capable and aware of mortal sins, he or she needs to confess those sins in the sacrament of Penance when possible.)

The Anointing of the Sick heals spiritually, and many times it heals physically. The roots of the sacrament can be found in the Letter of Saint James (Jas. 5:14–15) and of course in the ministry of Jesus Christ himself. Christ's whole life was one of healing and of reconciliation with our heavenly Father.

Priesthood is the vehicle whereby the life and ministry of Christ's life on earth is made present in today's world, through the seven sacraments. Nothing is implanted deeper in my mind when I am administering the sacrament of the sick. Most all priests have had numerous experiences of healing that could fill volumes. I have included a couple of illustrations which show facets of God's unfathomable love and mercy for his children through this sacrament.

A good friend called from the seminary one Saturday morning and said his mother was in the hospital, on a respirator, and not expected to live the weekend. He asked if I would rush over to the hospital and give her the Anointing of the Sick. I hurried over and indeed found her, unable to communicate because of the breathing machine, and looking as if she were close to death's door. I had known her for years and I had that sinking feeling that I probably would be doing a funeral in the not-too-distant future.

I did my priestly duty by anointing her and spent a little time trying to speak with her, then went back to the parish. I received a phone call the next day saying she had improved so much that she was being dismissed from the hospital that day. From death's door to home with family in one day! Now that is grace. That is a miracle. That is remarkable. That is God's love. Do you think maybe Our Lord wanted that mother present for her son's ordination to priesthood?

The likelihood of a priest being in our parish rectory on any Sunday afternoon or evening was negligible. Three priests were assigned to the parish and all of them took Sunday afternoons off to visit with their families. It was even more unusual for me to be there since I usually drove to my mother's home, one hundred miles south in central Virginia, returning the next evening after my day off.

Around 5:00 PM I received a call from the local emergency room, asking for a priest. One of our parishioners was suffering a major stroke. I rushed to the hospital and saw her.

She had confessed to me many times. She was so holy! Hearing her confession was "like being stoned with popcorn" to use an expression attributed to Venerable Fulton Sheen. What a lovely lady! I administered the Anointing of the Sick, granted her the Apostolic Pardon which is a non-contingent plenary indulgence given to those who are in grave danger of death. Soon I was on my way out of the hospital.

As I made it through one last door leading to the parking lot to head back to watch a Sunday football game, a nurse hailed me and directed me to the Coronary Care Unit. There was a Catholic man dying there and the staff wanted me to give him the last rites. Once again I anointed the patient and granted him the Apostolic Pardon. The nurse in the CCU informed me that person whom I had just anointed was a most generous man in his home country of Lebanon. He had built a number of orphanages for displaced children during that country's civil war, in the 1970s and 1980s.

Both the man and the woman died within six hours after they were anointed. Why was I called? Why was I in the rectory on that Sunday afternoon, for the first time in six months? God's grace! Our Lord wanted those two souls to be given special graces before he called them home. Both of these people were very special and Christ-like. Our Lord arranged the whole scenario so that he could bless his good disciples before he met them face-to-face. God will not be out done in generosity or love.

I received a call from a caregiver asking for a priest to come to see if he might help a terminally ill man. The patient was a young man of about thirty years of age and was dying of AIDS. The caregiver explained that the young man was close to death and might be hostile to a priest's presence. It had been many years since his patient had crossed the threshold of a church.

Upon hearing the term hostile, I was inspired to pray the Chaplet of Divine Mercy as I drove to see the dying man. When I arrived I found an emaciated form in bed, very sick indeed. I told him who I was and asked if I could hear his confession. It was difficult, almost impossible for him to speak, so I held his hand and asked that if he was sorry for his sins to please squeeze my hand. There was no hesitation on his part. He gave my hand a firm squeeze. I gave him absolution. God's mercy snatched a soul away from the evil one just in the nick of time.

"You are a priest forever." As a priest of Jesus Christ I have the privilege of doing every day what he did during his three years of public ministry; that is to heal, to forgive, and to make whole those souls desiring to enter into the eternal love of God. These examples of God's mercy flowing through his sacraments are just a sampling of his infinite love for his people. The examples are like so many grains of sand on the beach. The few that I have mentioned, wonderful as they are, are hardly visible when it comes to the magnitude, the enormity of the love and mercy our heavenly Father has for the people redeemed by his only Son Jesus Christ. The joy of priesthood grows deeper each and every day.

Priesthood

A New Life Begins

There is supposed to be a honeymoon, right? There usually is in marriage, in business relationships, in friendships, but not necessarily so in priesthood. Don't take me wrong; I was in love with priesthood and enjoyed settling into my first assignment. However, my honeymoon was over before I knew it had started.

At forty-two years of age I was the lone associate, the new priest on the block, for a pastor who was in his early seventies. Two other priests were living in the rectory, one who was medically retired, and another was a chancery man. That made four for dinner. The conversation was lively, with the pastor usually holding forth on most nights.

The cook had been in-place for almost twenty years and the pastor loved her. I did too, except for some of her practices in food preparation. Being a homebody, I would make my way into the kitchen in the afternoon, fix myself a cup of tea, and carry on a conversation with Doris, the name I hereby give to the cook. It became a habit of mine to spend some time with the cook of any parish to which I was assigned. I met and grew to love many nice ladies who tried their best to please the priests' palates.

On this particular day Doris was preparing spaghetti, and was adding the ground beef directly from the market package into the sauce. Silly me! I asked why she did not brown the meat first and then drain off the fat. She responded that she cooked the meat in the sauce to give the sauce more flavor. That was one of her secrets. I pursued this subject a bit more by asking if, after the meat had cooked in the sauce, she then skimmed the grease off of the top. She said that she did not; rather she stirred it back into the sauce for more flavor, of course. That was the last time I ever watched her cook. I thought it best that I did not know all of her secrets.

I had been ordained less than two months and had served in the parish for only half of that time, when I received a phone call one evening as I was leaving the dinner table. It was from a lady named Veronica, and although I only spoke to her briefly twice on the phone, a quarter of a century ago, I will never forget her. Veronica said that she called me specifically because I "had not had time to become hardened by years of service." I took a deep breath and said a silent prayer. I needed help.

The situation in which Veronica found herself was this. She was single and pregnant, her boyfriend was married, and she understood that having an abortion was the taking of a human life. Veronica loved life. She volunteered as a counselor at a pro-life agency. Complicating matters, the reason for the call to me, was a major predicament with her family and boyfriend. The boyfriend had given her a check for a thousand dollars and said, "Take care of it." Veronica's family told her that if she carried the baby to term, they would permanently ostracize her.

Veronica indicated that she was losing weight rather than gaining it, due to the emotional and spiritual struggle that this pregnancy created. She understood that she was carrying a baby, and she knew that her parents were serious about ostracizing her. She felt totally alone, abandoned by her family as well as by the boyfriend. She told me, "I am weak, Father, and I need my family."

What was she to do? I offered all the support I could think of, including a place to stay nearby or out of town, financial help, emotional help, and of course, spiritual assistance. Adoption was discussed as an option. This was years before national programs such as Project Rachel or Project Gabriel were in place.

Veronica called on a Tuesday evening. The abortion was set for Friday morning. Before hanging up she indicated that she would consider everything I had said and that she would stay in touch. Veronica also said, "I can have the abortion and then go to confession." I reminded her that that would be presumption. We concluded the conversation with her understanding that help would be offered for anything she needed regarding the pregnancy, for herself and/or for the child. It would be an understatement to say that she was emotionally distraught.

I was assigned the early morning Mass for the next day, so I went to bed early. Less than an hour later the phone woke me up out of a dead sleep. It was Veronica. After our earlier conversation, the abortion mill called her with the news of an appointment cancellation for later the same evening. They offered her the open slot. She had the abortion. I have never to this day heard anyone so upset on the other end of a phone. Half asleep, I do remember asking her if I could help, if I could hear her confession. "NO!" was her answer, and the conversation ended.

This happened on a Tuesday. Friday of the same week I received a letter from a friend of hers notifying me that Veronica committed suicide sometime after the late night phone call to me. The letter accused me of causing her suicide because of my "lack of love and compassion."

The same Friday evening, a healing Mass had been scheduled with Fr. John Lubey presiding. Fr. Lubey had a solid local reputation for healing and for reading souls. While in the sacristy preparing for the healing Mass, I asked and received a blessing from Fr. Lubey. A moment before we processed down the aisle, Fr. Lubey called me over to him and said, "Don't be upset; you don't have all the answers yet." Amazing! I had not uttered a word about the suicide to anyone and yet he had addressed my heartfelt concern. I came to know him well over the next decade as an outstanding and holy priest.

So there you have it, the end of my honeymoon in priesthood. It was an important lesson on the tactics of the devil. Additionally it was a heartfelt loss, from which I have never completely recovered.

Positively speaking, I became a pro-life activist, not to say that all priests are not. Some of my quests in life became, and still are, to change society's stance on abortion, to help ladies who are in difficult pregnancies, and to comfort and heal those who have been victimized by this awful form of domestic violence. The death of the pre-born by this brutal, demonic industry must be stopped. I hope and pray that we may finally muster an army of ten million strong pro-lifers to show society how sick, selfish, and demented we have become through this murderous practice. It has become the true downfall of our great nation.

As of this writing, we have aborted over fifty-three million children in this country, more persons that the total population of the ten largest cities in our country combined. Imagine those cities empty!

My ordination was at the hands of the Most Rev. John R. Keating, Bishop of Arlington. He was a holy man and a great bishop. I remember meeting him for the first time when I was in second theology, during his annual visit to the Mount. I was so anxious that by the time he came into my immediate presence, I had a difficult time speaking clearly and I stuttered badly. He just looked at me and moved on without saying a word. I worried for many months about whether he would allow my ordination.

I have always been grateful to Bishop Keating for ordaining me even though he was well aware of my speech difficulties two years before the ordination. He took a chance; I think it may have paid off in the long run, even if I did have to take a medical retirement after twenty-one years in active ministry.

In August of 1986, three months after ordination, I was hearing an after-hours confession in the rectory office. A lady, in her mid-thirties, was confessing as usual when she started to stammer and look uneasy. She began to act out of character, and expressed negative thoughts about confession and such.

I asked her what was wrong and if she had finished with the confessing of sins. She said that she had one more sin to confess, but that "it" would not let her. Strange indeed! I asked who or what was the "it" that would not let her complete the confession. Then all hell seemed to break loose. Her color became very flushed with pinks and reds. While she was in this agitated state, I asked again who or what it was that would not let her confess. She looked at me with bulging eyes and said in a deep voice, "You don't scare me any, you young priest, Ha, ha, ha." Praying deliverance prayers to the best of my ability, I asked Saint Michael to help, and for guidance from the Holy Spirit. I had not been prepared for this type of combat. The seminary seemed to have skipped lessons in Demonology 101. I was sort of flattered that "it" called me a young priest. It was right. While I was chronologically forty-two years old, I was only ninety days a priest. After twenty minutes or so the lady came back to herself and finished the confession.

This began a year-long situation which culminated with my petitioning Bishop Keating for permission to perform an exorcism. In the meanwhile, in preparation for the decision to exorcise this woman, the bishop told me to accompany Dorothy (not her real name) to pray separately with three persons of his choosing in the diocese. Two of these persons were known for their holiness, while the third was a psychiatrist. I was not looking forward to these sessions.

Before approaching the bishop, I had a priest friend come by and pray with Dorothy and me. Once again, for the umpteenth time, she displayed demonic personalities. She would really drain the energy out of me. That entire year I walked around like a zombie (no relation to her personalities) because of her constant presence in my life.

The priest friend, who later became a hermit, was convinced of the reality of demonic possession. Over the year I came to know much of her life in detail. She grew up on the fringes of her class in high school. In order to make herself feel wanted, influential, and powerful, Dorothy began to dabble in the occult. She was first introduced to Ouija boards, then tarot cards, and then séances. All of these have evil origins. They seem to be innocent games, but they are not! They are directly from Satan.

These games allowed evil to form a wedge into her heart and soul. She expressed to me how she could wish evil upon people, and then evil would actually happen to them. People began to notice her with regard to the occult, and this played to her wounded ego. She came back to church, but evil had a hold on her and was not letting go easily.

The first of the three to pray with Dorothy and me was the psychiatrist. After praying with us for a half-hour, and trying to observe her as well, the psychiatrist left my office in a hurry, almost running, and told me as he was leaving, "There is not a doubt, she is possessed." However, when he wrote his report for Bishop Keating, he hedged and wrote that it was a possible possession.

My spiritual director, an older priest who had been ordained for fifty years, was the second person to pray with us. He was doubtful and said possible possession.

The third person was the abbot of a Trappist monastery. We had an interview with him for about a half-hour, during which Dorothy was perfectly normal. Then as we were getting ready to leave she began to exhibit demonic behaviors as described earlier. The abbot sat us back down and began to perform the rite of exorcism over Dorothy for more than three hours. He called it a deliverance prayer, because he did not have the permission of the bishop in hand. Meanwhile, I was sprinkling her with holy water and asking the intercession of the saints and angels. The abbot definitely considered Dorothy to be possessed.

The prayers and the sprinkling with holy water seemed to bother and upset the demons, but in the end, when Dorothy had regained control of herself, she still had the same problems as before. I could not say whether the demons' strength had decreased due to the session, but they were still there. I was exhausted and was delighted that the whole thing was over for the time being. It is because of this experience that I began the practice of holding a crucifix in my hands while sleeping, and I have not abandoned the practice.

All of these events finally led to a meeting with the bishop. At last I was going to be told whether Dorothy was to be the recipient of the Rite of Exorcism. Those prayer sessions were like something out of classic movies. There was no head turning around or Cinema-style effects, but they were not picnics either. As I sat in his office, along with the diocesan Chancellor, Bishop Keating asked if I believed in angels. I said, "Yes" and he responded that that was a good answer, because their existence is a doctrine of the church.

If there are no angels, then there is no devil. If the devil does not exist, then Adam and Eve were not tempted to eat the apple. If Adam and Eve did not eat the apple, then they did not sin. If they did not sin, then we do not suffer the consequences of original sin. If we do not suffer the consequence of original sin, then we do not need a redeemer. If we do not need a redeemer, then we do not need Jesus Christ. It is like proving the domino effect theory.

Bishop Keating said that he had prayed and fasted all weekend for Dorothy and me. His decision was this: he wanted to see one level of possession higher than she had shown up to then. I asked what this might be and he said the signs he was looking for were levitation, supernatural strength, or supernatural knowledge. Until one of those was manifested, the bishop told me to disassociate myself from her.

Praise God! Dorothy never showed any of these signs of possession. With feelings of relief that the ordeal was over, but still concerned for her welfare, I broke off communication with Dorothy. She was definitely obsessed with evil spirits, and heavily so, but not possessed. She still managed some control over her personhood. Breaking off communication with her was a blessing, but it was also difficult. It was a blessing because I was able to regain an increase in my energy level, but difficult because a caring, empathetic relationship had formed and the bishop's orders were to let it drop.

This encounter with Bishop Keating went a long way to seal an already present admiration for him. He told me that he had fasted and prayed all weekend for Dorothy and me because he wanted to make the right decision, and he thought fasting and praying was the way to do it. Imagine that, a bishop taking time to fast and pray for one parishioner! He was a quiet man, but praying and fasting for one person is above the call to duty. This looks like holiness to me. What love he showed by doing this, and what a great example he was to me as well.

All priests have encounters with evil, and many have had a good deal more serious encounters than what I have described. While this was my first, it certainly was not the last of my close-up battles with the creep from down below. Welcome to the priesthood of Jesus Christ!

After Mass on the first Sunday of September, during my fourth month as a priest, someone asked me about RCIA. RCIA what? I knew it was a new name for inquiry classes, but I had no clue as to its format, content, how to run the program, or anything else about it. Clueless? Yes indeed, I was clueless! I was not even sure what the initials meant. For all I knew they could have stood for Roman Catholic Intelligence Agency. Actually, they stand for Rite of Christian Initiation of Adults. You knew that, didn't you?

The next evening, I asked the pastor about it. He said his previous associate, who was now in the Army, had run an Inquiry Class, which always started in September. It was already September; was I ever behind! I was under the gun and just a trifle nervous about teaching. I had never taught a class in my life!

Thank God for well-informed priest friends! I called around and learned of a great author, Alan Schreck, a professor from Franciscan University at Steubenville, Ohio. He published a catechism that was easy to read, yet comprehensively covered the basics of the faith. In fact that is the title: *Basics of the Faith, a Catholic Catechism*. It is so orthodox, that is, loyal to Rome, that it squeaks. The author, Alan Schreck, has updated the same good book, but now it is published under the title of *The Essential Catholic Catechism.*

Over time I found that I enjoyed teaching. After a rough start, I became at least adequate in teaching the faith to others. So began a twenty-one year history of teaching most of the RCIA classes in whatever parish assignment I happened to be. Sometimes we ran two sessions per year. I found it difficult to tell people, "Wait until September," when someone in December or January inquired into the possibility of becoming Catholic. So we often started a new class in January.

In September of 1986, when that very first RCIA class was over, I was momentarily the happiest priest in the diocese. I was already scarred and battle weary, but I had made it through. My mindset going into the class was simply to take charge, do what I could do, and survive. Yes, it was my first teaching assignment ever. It was a new parish. It was full of strangers, and yes, I was incredibly nervous. Nevertheless, Jesus had gotten me this far and I knew he was not going to abandon me now.

The evening of that first class, I was introduced to a couple of personality types previously unknown to me. The seminary did not prepare us for them, either. They were the angry Catholics and the heterodox Catholics, whose mission it was to change the church from within. In reality, the latter were protestant, but for some reason still to be revealed, continued to attend the Catholic church. They were protestant in a Catholic shell.

I had been teaching the class for about ten minutes when someone raised his hand and asked, in a less-than-friendly tone, why the church did not allow women priests. He went on to express dismay about our prohibition of the use of artificial contraception, about divorce and remarriage, and about a host of other hot button issues of the day.

I was floored! I did not know what to do. Should I take time and answer these attacks? Where should I start? Should I dismiss them? Should I? Should I? Should I? Was this what teaching RCIA was all about? I had had enough and the first class was only fifteen minutes old! What was going on? Mercifully, Our Lord had placed a few wonderful parishioners in the class, and they began to come to my defense. They were articulate and loyal Catholics, through and through. Thanks for the troops, Lord!

The troops gathered around me after class and gave me much needed encouragement and a little direction, too. With their help, much inspiration from sitting with the Blessed Sacrament, and some study, I became the respectable teacher that Our Lord knew I would become. It did require some growing pains, though.

As I think back over twenty-one years as an active parish priest, I can count hundreds of converts from those RCIA classes. Many more cradle Catholics received sacraments that they had missed along the way, and numerous other Catholics came to know and appreciate their faith in a deeper way. The beginning was anything but promising. Fortitude does count, as does having a deep abiding understanding of God's love and presence in one's life and priesthood.

Those angry Catholics, together with cafeteria types, blended in with a few progressives, can make the life of a priest a field of humility and humiliation, as well as a testing ground for the practice of virtue. Our job, if you call priesthood a job (it is a vocation), is to help all God's children attain everlasting life in heaven. However, many of these disgruntled folk make us priests work on perfecting virtue in our own lives, here and now. We try to be like Christ, in whose priesthood we share, but most of us priests have gigantic hills to climb before we come close to imitating him. Maybe this is why Our Lord sends us an assorted flock to work with.

Why does the church experience large numbers of these disgruntled members? After wrestling with this question most of my active ministry, the answer became crystal clear from a statement from the Holy Father himself. Pope Benedict XVI says that the reason the church finds herself with dwindling numbers of active Catholics as well as dissention from church teaching and her authority is attributable to the poor catechetical programs offered in the church for the past forty years.

During those first few months in priesthood, I also became aware of a new way of using the terms zinger and barb. These are usually one-liners, used by a small but vocal minority of parishioners as they greet the priest after Sunday Mass. At the end of Mass, the priest recesses out the back of church to greet the congregants as they leave, wish them well, and enjoy some small talk, all very friendly, of course.

Nonetheless, during what should be a rather joyful assembly of God's holy people, the priest needs to steel himself for the inevitable. One can never tell where it is going to come from, the zinger that is, but it was coming to be sure. Supportive parishioners will say good-by and thank the celebrant for being a priest or for giving a good homily. Then this ordinary-looking, seemingly friendly parishioner will approach and lay a bombshell on him. He, or she, will be angry or disappointed with the homily, the way the church is decorated, the interior temperature of the church, the flowers, the candles, you name it.

An associate-pastor learns quickly enough to simply refer most of these comments to the pastor. When I became a pastor myself, I learned how unpleasant it was to field what soon enough became troublesome, but routine, inquiries or complaints.

Often they were personal zingers such as, "Why are you always so negative, Father? Don't you know we come to church to be uplifted?" Some uttered complaints about me for speaking on the topic of abortion too often, or offered such advice as telling me to get with it because I frequently expressed the necessity of frequenting the sacrament of Penance. These are really mild zingers. Some were worse, but I am sure you get the drift.

The worst comment I heard was directed to an associate of mine. He had only been ordained three months when a woman approached him after Mass and said, "Father, you are a cancer on our parish." That one was the worst, but there are many others that run a close second in the trash department. Do these people think that we should all be made in their image and likeness? The insulted priest handled the barb well, outwardly at least.

Occasionally, the parishioners who offered priests these challenges could be won over to orthodoxy, that is, adherence to the true teaching of the church. This was not always the case, but attempts to do so were required of us. Sometimes it simply meant a one-on-one visit, with a display of compassion and patience from the priest. Sometimes it required a few lively discussions about the truths of the faith. If the parishioners were open-minded there was hope for a conversion of these thorns in our sides. If success was to be, prayer was always a part of the equation.

All the above, from the letter accusing me of causing a suicide, to the dealing with demonic possession issues, to learning how to teach, to the handling of zingers, were all part of learning how to live the life of a parish priest. There is much more to the daily routine, including rectory living, keeping up one's spiritual life, working with pre-Cana, funerals, giving spiritual direction, counseling of all types, working with youth groups, making visits to elderly and shut-ins, *etc. etc.* If a priest loves the church and Jesus Christ, his life is never boring.

The following is an anecdote from those years of teaching RCIA that I found to be humorous as well as a beautiful example of the lengths to which Our Lord will go to bring us all back to him.

A man pushing fifty years of age strolled into the first session of an RCIA class. He had no intention of paying attention to anything I said. His only interest was to be close to his live-in girlfriend, who wanted to know a little more about the faith into which she was born. This couple would sit in the back of the room making eyes at each other and drinking root beer. This nonsense went on week after week until the word abortion was mentioned. Then his ears perked up and he took an active interest in the class material.

This guy was outraged at the church's position on abortion, citing the stereotypical rape and incest argument. However, he came around to embrace our understanding of eternal truth. This live-in boyfriend became a Catholic, and the couple was married in the church. Additionally, the man's adult children from a previous marriage, as well as his grandchildren, were received into the church. The pebble cast into the waters of life does cause ripples and the ripples continue.

Each of us, no matter who we are, has an effect on others. Everyone, from the elderly who are in assisted care facilities, to the most active priest, all affect one another for good or bad. If we embrace Christ by trying to live as he teaches, we will bring people to him. Sometimes we see the effects we have on people, and at other times we do not.

Many of us do not realize that, no matter how hidden our lives may be, we can be very effective disciples for Our Lord. I have heard time and again how useless nuns are, especially those religious who live behind cloistered walls. People say things such as, "Why don't they go out into the world and work with the poor or something, instead of wasting time behind those walls? Don't they know they are living in the past?"

We are all members of the Body of Christ, and what one does behind closed walls has an effect on the whole Body of Christ. If one member is praising God, doing acts of penance, praying for other members of the Mystical Body of Christ, and trying to become more pleasing to Our Lord himself, then he, or she, helps the whole Body. So if we find ourselves basically alone in life, we need to remember that we are very much loved by Our Lord and can have a positive effect on the whole Body by working on our own holiness of life issues. What we do in secret will be made public.

The opposite is also true. The more sinful we are, the more we hurt the whole Body of Christ. If I fall down and break my arm, that injury has a negative effect on the rest of my body. The same holds true with the Body of Christ. If I am sinful I hurt others as well.

I am convinced that when we meet Our Lord Jesus Christ, he will show each of us a review of our lives, and we will be enlightened as to the many people we have affected by our lives. In other words, we will see the ripple effect that our efforts to imitate Christ has had on other souls in this life. That is something to ponder. It helps to give meaning even to our loneliest of days.

Taking care of daily duties in itself brings people to Christ. It makes no difference whether anyone sees the duties being carried out, or even knows of them. All of those unborn children we have prayed for, all of those relatives we have prayed for, all of those holy intentions that we have lifted up God, and all of those struggles against our own sins will not go for naught. Our Lord knows and he allows the merits of our good life, struggles and all, to go for his honor and glory, and for our salvation.

Priesthood does indeed have a lighter side. Of course! I can think of nothing more humorous than a few episodes which involved my first pastor. He did not have a mean bone in his body, but we priests sometimes need to laugh at ourselves and at each other. God rest his soul.

My first Christmas as a priest, I fielded the first phone call in which someone asked me, "What time is your Midnight Mass?" Until then I always thought that was a joke of some kind! But it is true! People do call to ask the time of Midnight Mass. Ours was always at midnight but my pastor took one of those calls and answered, "Midnight Mass is at eleven-fifty-nine-and-a-half PM." The caller did not understand, so the pastor had to repeat his answer three times! Frustrated, he finally hung up on the dear lady. I wonder if she was on time or went to another church.

That same season held one more amusing anecdote involving my pastor. The chancery priest was saying Mass, and the rest of us priests were waiting in the sacristy, vested and ready to distribute Holy Communion. The crotchety, medically retired priest noticed that the good pastor had on a green stole with red fringe at the bottom. Said Crotchety to the pastor, "The Mass calls for a white stole," to which the pastor replied, "But green and red are the colors of the season." The pastor changed to a white stole, but he gave us his famous frown look, stomped his feet, and was in a mood the rest of the evening. Crotchety and I had a good laugh that we shared for years to come over that issue. I'm still smiling as I recall those characters.

I came to find out that the pastor's stomping his feet episode was not unusual. One evening while the chancery priest was absent from dinner, Crotchety and I carried on a longer than usual dinner conversation. The pastor was not able to break into the conversation, so he stood up, walked to the dining room door, wiped his mouth with his napkin, gave us a grimaced glance, stomped his feet, and left the room, never to appear again that evening.

One evening, a classmate, a brother priest of the same diocese called. Fr. Pastor answered and, when questioned as to my whereabouts, replied, "Oh, he's in church, in ecstasy." Then he hung up. I thought it was funny, and so did my classmate.

I wonder sometimes what sort of stories circulate about me among former associates. I hope they treat me as kindly as I was treated by my first pastor. He allowed me to indulge myself in pet projects to my heart's content. I was allowed to start and maintain a Wednesday evening Mass in honor of Our Lady, Queen of Peace, and institute a Eucharistic Holy Hour with confessions on Friday evenings. Both practices continued until I left that fine parish. I thank him for allowing me the freedom to carry on what I still think are wonderful devotions.

The Eucharistic Holy Hour was, and is, a favorite of mine. I think all parishes nationwide, worldwide, should have a night devoted to the Blessed Sacrament weekly. We also need more Eucharistic adoration chapels, and we need to multiply the times and days for confessions throughout the universal church. The congregations need to know how important these sacraments are to their daily lives in their struggle to get to heaven.

The transition from the seminary to the priesthood involved a massive learning curve. It was both exciting and revealing: exciting to be a priest and revealing of self and of others. I began to learn much about the human person, of our brokenness and of our dreams.

The foregoing were the most difficult tasks that first year, other than the continual struggle with speech issues. The latter diminished as time wore on, especially as I grew deeper in the understanding that I am a priest of Jesus Christ, forever.

It is mystifying how a problem that occupied my mind for decades faded into comparative oblivion when meatier matters in priesthood came along after ordination. The stuttering issue came about through a violent eruption of evil, a clear lack of love. Some of the hurtful incidents in my life may have just been attempts at bad humor; I guess I will find out on judgment day. Still, this lack of love was driven by anger, hatred, jealousy, and misplaced bigotry. Who can survive in a world like that? Not me! Praise God, it dissipated. Through love itself, the issue of stuttering receded from my consciousness as being a major issue. The unconditional love of our Creator and Redeemer for his children transformed this lowly being into a new person. I was reborn in love to be his priest.

I would not trade one of these experiences for all the tea in China, to use an old expression. I believe they helped form me into becoming a better priest, as do all difficult days in life. There is nothing like on-the-job training. To know that God is always with me is my greatest treasure, and it is the most powerful weapon I possess.

Sometimes Jesus Christ chooses the least likely, in the eyes of the world, to be priests. He makes priests out of such unworthy material to ensure that those priests will always know they have nothing to boast about except the mercy of Christ. All of us priests must be forever grateful for his love and mercy. Mercy shown to us compels us to show Christ's love and mercy to his people.

Betania

My brother-in-law Charlie was dying of bone cancer. The only hope he had of surviving was to be miraculously healed by heavenly intervention. My first thought was to help him make a pilgrimage. I recalled hearing of Marian apparitions taking place in Venezuela, two hours distant from Caracas, on the side of a mountain called Betania. The apparitions had the approval of the local bishop, thus providing an important assurance of the authenticity of such events. Over my years of active ministry, I traveled to many pilgrim destinations throughout the world. I have chosen to share some thoughts and experiences regarding Betania. Why Betania and not another Marian shrine? Betania' apparitions are both current and are approved by the local bishop. The church usually stays mum on the subject of apparitions unless the messages coming from them are contrary to church teaching. For instance, the "apparitions" in Bayside, New York, have been condemned because the messages are contrary to the teachings of the church's magisterium. I was also honored to meet and interact with the Betania visionary several times. Additionally, members of my family and friends have experienced an assortment of healings on our pilgrimages there.

I should have known that Our Lady had planned something wonderful for us on that first trip to Betania. There were so many obstacles to overcome before Charlie, my sister Mary Lou, and myself ever even got to the airport. The devil knows what is going on in the real world and will do everything to discourage and defeat what he thinks may the occasion for a glorious outpouring of God's grace.

There was the case of the strange illness with which I was afflicted with strange symptoms for five nights preceding our flight to Caracas. After dinner I experienced severe chills such as I have never had before. This went on for several hours each night. It was strange! Adding more stress to the situation, there was the incident of being stuck at a mountain cabin thirty-six hours before the trip. This takes a little explanation.

Mary Lou, Charlie, and I were supposed to fly out of Reagan National Airport on Tuesday morning. After changing planes in Miami we were to meet up with some other pilgrims and our guides. For three weeks prior to our planned trip, the weather had been brutally severe in northern Virginia. We had ice storms, freezing rain, and record-setting low temperatures. This all combined to make me worry about my family cottage which stood close to the top of the highest mountain in the Blue Ridge Range, outside of Skyline Drive. The Sunday before the trip was the last chance to check up on things before leaving the country. We're talking rough mountains here. I needed to see if any pipes had frozen or burst, make sure no branch had fallen through the roof (it had happened before), make sure the heat still worked, etc.

To complicate matters, I had asked the rectory cook to ride with me. She was a wonderful lady, about thirty years my senior. We both thought we would be back in time to watch the Super Bowl the same evening. I went up the mountain in my 4-wheel drive Chevy Blazer just fine, but as

I approached my driveway, which went down a sharp slope to the parking area, I noticed what appeared to be a thin coating of snow on the drive. The road could not have been more than thirty yards down the hill with a slight turn to the left. I started down the hill tentatively, but as all four wheels hit the slope, the car took off as if it had a mind of its own. "It is ice, you dummy!" I said to myself. Instead of a thin coating of snow, the drive was coated with about an inch of ice! That was the quickest and scariest thirty yards I have ever driven. Not only was the car out of control, but also if it had continued to travel on the same trajectory, we would have slammed broadside into a fat and healthy three-story oak tree! Suddenly, just as it was going to make impact with the tree, the car swerved on its own to the left, coming to a halt, finally obeying the breaking and steering I thought I was applying all the time. No one can convince me that luck had anything to do with our escaping that tree. It had to have been divine intervention, probably my guardian angel. Thank you angel of God, my guardian dear!

After recovering our senses, the housekeeper and I had a good laugh! Then reality set in. I tried to turn the car around in the driveway. No way! Every time I tried to turn the car, it would edge closer to the brink of the parking area. If we had gone over the edge, the car would have fallen about fifty yards down the mountain and crashed into some large boulders and trees. It was scary!

Because I was unable to turn the car around, I tried to back up the drive to the main road. After moving about ten yards up the hill, I continued in reverse, but the car began to inch forward even though the wheels were churning backwards. Then the car shifted on the ice, sending the front right wheel over the small rock border of the driveway, and the car aimed itself at the house, only a few precious feet away. So there we sat! If I had tried to move the car at all, it would have slid into my cabin. We were stuck! High on a mountain with icy roads, three miles off the main road, eighty miles away from the rectory, we had no way to go anywhere.

We went inside the cottage and, thank God, the phone (this was before mobile communication devices) and heat both worked. I called AAA. After waiting, and waiting, they called us back and informed us that the wrecker could not climb the mountain because the roads had become too icy. What was I to do now? I called the priest from the local parish, Saint John the Baptist in Front Royal, Virginia. The pastor was home, and he brightened our outlook by reminding me of a parishioner who lived a quarter-mile further up my road. We called my neighbor-parishioner, who agreed to try to get us down the mountain to the main road. Then the son-in-law of the housekeeper agreed to travel the eighty miles from his home and pick us up.

That embarrassing moment was not over; it had a final flourish before finally ending on a good note. The son-in-law did not want to come and pick us up until after the Super Bowl game. This made it difficult for the parishioner, because as the evening progressed the mountain got colder and the roads got icier. (The easy part for the neighbor was getting us down to our ride. Getting back up the mountain and back home again, I am sure, was even more troublesome.) Nevertheless, we got down the hill and I got off to Betania on Tuesday. I am sure that there was talk in that mountain parish over the next few weeks about the priest and his housekeeper who had to be rescued at eleven o'clock at night, after watching the Super Bowl. Oh well.

Betania is in an agricultural area approximately two hours by bus from Caracas, Venezuela's capital. Tropical, mountainous, and close to the rain forests, the vegetation is lush and beautiful. Typical of Venezuela, the populace are poor but friendly, a happy people. The birds are exotic and numerous. The weather is warm all year.

The Blessed Virgin Mary has been appearing in Betania since March 25, 1976, first to the mystic Maria Esperanza De Bianchini. Maria Esperanza is Spanish for Mary Hope. However the visionary Maria is not the only person to have seen her there. The local bishop has stated that many people, as many as ten thousand, have seen the Blessed Virgin Mary. Betania has been called the Lourdes of the West because many people have been cured by drinking its waters or by putting the water on the affected areas of their bodies. The water is from a natural spring next to the grotto where the Blessed Mother has appeared. The spring water flows down the hillside, making a natural waterfall.

We brought some of the water home and freely gave it away. A friend of a family member, a non-believer, was cured of arthritis in his shoulder by applying the water to the affected area. He was amazed, as were we. A non-believer! I wish I had been able to track this non-believer's faith journey since the cure.

I liken Betania to an exquisite multi-faceted diamond. In addition to the healing waters, a eucharistic miracle occurred there on December 8, 1991. During a Mass, the host, which the priest had consecrated and was to be consumed by him, began to bleed while on the paten, before he raised it to declare, "This is the Lamb of God who takes away the sins of the world. Happy are those called to his supper." (Old translation.) There is actual footage of this event taken by a pilgrim on his camcorder, distinctly showing the host bleeding. The host was tested later and the lab report said that it was human flesh.

The Blessed Virgin Mary appears to hundreds of pilgrims at a time. During a single apparition, she may appear differently to individual pilgrims who are standing side by side. I think this is a first with regard to apparitions of Our Lady. She may appear as Our Lady of Grace, Our Lady of Fatima, Our Lady of Perpetual Help, or under one of the many other titles by which she is known and loved. If this would be publicized throughout the Americas, I think it would make Betania a more popular pilgrim destination.

There are numerous visible and tangible signs of God's love for his people at Betania. We, in this modern world, tend to be skeptical of miraculous signs and events such as those occurring at Betania. In the gospel of John, Jesus says that you can only produce spiritual fruit when in you are in union with him. Some of the fruits of Betania are: people cured of disease, thousands drawn closer to Our Lord through Our Lady, healings of relationships, and improved attitudes and outlooks on life. The list of incredible signs of God's love for the human person continues. Betania is one of those special places where God goes outside of normal channels to draw us to his infinite love. We ourselves are the stumbling blocks.

Betania is the country home of Maria Esperanza, her private estate. She bought the property under the direction of the Virgin Mary, who foretold the many supernatural events which would occur there. Maria was so gracious that she opened the site to anyone wishing to come in peace.

Maria was a mere eleven years old when she had her first mystical experience, but that was only the beginning. Our Lord set her apart for a difficult but privileged life of daily interaction with the supernatural, having visions and locutions of Jesus, Mary, and various other saints. She was a very joyful person, consistently stressing the mercy of Jesus and his infinite love for mankind.

Maria was married in Saint Peters Vatican Basilica, in Rome. It was on that trip that she went to southern Italy and met Saint Pio of Pietrelcina. Padre Pio told her his time on earth was coming to an end and that she had to carry on his work. Indeed, Maria did have many of the same spiritual gifts which Padre Pio possessed. All during her life she had these supernatural gifts, while at the same time delicately balancing being a dedicated wife and mother. Maria died in August of 2006. Having met her several times and witnessed her work, I believe her cause will continue to go forward for canonization.

One of her gifts was that of bi-location. I was with Maria when her husband testified about an evening when she had laid her head on his shoulder while watching TV and went to sleep. At that same moment in time, hundreds of people later testified that she had been in front of a large audience miles away, speaking to them about the Blessed Virgin Mary. How is that for a spouse!

Maria was also united to Christ through profound, personal sufferings. She suffered his Passion on Good Fridays, and maybe at other times as well. This passion included the visible stigmata, the five wounds of Christ's crucifixion. I witnessed her suffering from a stigmatic wound on her left hand as she interceded with heavenly powers to cure me of spiritual and physical issues.

Many persons familiar with the spiritual life have heard of the gifts described thus far. However, heaven provided Maria with a bizarre but beautiful gift, one that I think is peculiar to her alone.

On occasion, Maria would suffer what appeared to be a heart attack. Her chest would physically open and a living rose, complete with drops of dew on the petals, and thorns on the stem, would come out from her chest. I said it was unusual and very hard to believe, but it is true. The roses were vehicles, instruments, of healing. I was a witness to some of these healings.

Bishop Pio Bello of the Diocese of Los Teques in the state of Miranda, in whose diocese Betania is located, wrote a pastoral letter, dated November 21, 1987, regarding the apparitions in Betania. The letter spoke of the findings of his ecclesiastical investigation of the apparitions that began on March 25, 1984. The pastoral letter was positive. It found the apparitions to be true and fruitful in the lives of those people who have seen Our Lady and even for those who have not seen her but have been helped because of their pilgrimage to the apparition site.

The hope for a miraculous cure of Charlie's bone cancer was the primary purpose of the trip, but countless other graces came from the trip, which were totally unexpected, as another display of God's affection for us.

Arriving at our hotel in Caracas, we were told that Maria Esperanza was not in Betania, but in New Jersey. (New Jersey is a lot closer to Reagan National Airport than is Caracas.) Our hearts sank. Knowing of her spiritual gifts, we were positive that she was supposed to be the vehicle through whom Charlie was going to be cured, and she was in New Jersey. Now what? Well, we continued with our pilgrimage, of course, but our spirits had taken a blow.

We arrived at the hotel that first day around 2:00 PM. No meal was served on the plane and nothing was available in the hotel until dinner, so Charlie and I went to explore Caracas to find a bite to eat, something to hold us over until dinner. We discovered a store that sold already-prepared sandwiches and pastries, which looked truly inviting to two starving pilgrims, so we went in to try our luck at purchasing a few ham-and-cheese sandwiches to go. It didn't help that neither of us spoke Spanish. In this store you were to go to the cashier at the counter in the center of the room, place your order and pay for it, then take the receipt to a clerk standing behind the display counter, who would fill your order.

Well, it didn't work out that way for us. Thinking back, the events that unfolded in that store had to be of divine intervention, in a most humorous but practical way. Trying to purchase the food items, I pointed to the sandwiches in the glass case and held up three fingers to indicate the quantity. I then gave the cashier twenty American dollars as I recall, thinking that had to be sufficient for three ham-and-cheese sandwiches that had been sitting under the glass, probably for hours. The clerk took the money, rang something up in the cash register and gave me a receipt and some change. I took the receipt over to the counter where I expected to receive the sandwiches. Not yet! The clerk refused to give me what I thought I had paid for. Evidently there was a lack of communication between the cashier and me, and I had failed to pay for what I had intended.

Frustrated and feeling those hunger pains, I began to raise my voice to the clerk, in English of course, so he responded by raising his voice back to me in Spanish. So there we were, two starving Americans in the capital of Venezuela, having a shouting match with a clerk in a store. If I had not been so tired I would have probably thought the whole affair to be comical. But at that point, in my frustration, I yelled something like, "God help me!"

Instantly, I was aware of a huge construction worker standing next to me. In perfect English he asked if he could help. I tried to explain the situation about attempting to purchase three lousy ham-and-cheese sandwiches and being denied them by the clerk. He went to the counter, and in perfect Spanish, told the clerk to give me the sandwiches. Reluctantly, but afraid of my new friend, probably because of his physical size, the clerk gave me the sandwiches. The construction worker turned back to me, and again in perfect English, asked if I wanted anything else. I thanked him and indicated that I was most satisfied to possess those sandwiches, and Charlie and I were on our way back to the hotel.

We thought it was great that someone helped us, and we devoured our food, but gave no thought as to who the construction worker was, how he just happened to be next to me when I needed special help, or that he just happened to speak perfect English and Spanish, too. We were delighted just to have our simple food.

Only later, after the pilgrimage was over, did I guess that my construction worker friend might have been an angel. It seems odd to be shopping in a Spanish-culture city and to have a construction worker, who is fluent in two languages, instantly appear next to you. Especially because he had no apparent accent in either language. Being multilingual without any accent is not a normal characteristic of construction workers. He was huge, the better to demand what I wanted, and he was very clean, unusually so for a construction worker in the middle of a large city. The man was most accommodating to the priest, too! I truly think he was my guardian angel. Nothing else makes sense. What a wonderful way to take care of his crazy priest! I am grateful! That was neither the first nor the last time he has helped me out when I needed him.

Remember when I spoke about the phenomena of Maria's chest opening and a rose coming out? Maria had given our tour guide, Wendy Benedict, several of those rose petals. Wendy reminded me that Maria said the roses are a gift from heaven and are instruments of healing. Through God's grace I found myself open to this unusual channel of his love, so I took one of the petals and went off to my room and, while holding the petal in my hands, I asked the Blessed Virgin for a number of intercessory favors. I remember praying for my parish and for healings of various peoples. After the pilgrimage was over and I was back in the parish, I heard astonishing stories of healings from persons I had lifted up in prayer.

A retired priest, incardinated in a different diocese, was

living with his family within the boundaries of our parish. He had previously helped us out with confessions and celebrating a Mass or two on weekends whenever his health permitted. My trip was in late January and early February of 1994. The previous October, the retired priest had a serious falling-out with my pastor. During my pilgrimage to Betania, he called the pastor and reconciled sufficiently to begin helping in the parish again. To think that that reconciliation was not due to heavenly intervention would be unreasonable.

Satan noticed that we had a thriving youth group in our parish. So he went to work in the summer of 1993, and created a nasty split among the most active of the families involved. It was a major break-up with about four families on one side of the debate and five families on the other. The division was so deep that the pastor believed the only way to settle things was to disband the group. However the Blessed Mother came to the rescue.

The parents of the children involved in the group had a meeting the same weekend I was in Betania, reconciled differences, and effected a healing. Once again, the youth group was restored to being an active part of the parish community. Thanks to Our Lady, the graces were there to heal and reconcile. Thank you, Mother.

The Blessed Virgin Mary told Maria Esperanza that she wished to be known as Reconciler of Peoples and of Nations. With the above two examples from my parish, it is easy to see that our heavenly Mother lives up to that worthy title. Just as at the wedding feast at Cana two thousand years ago, she continues to look out for her sons and daughters in every age. We can always count on Our Lady for intercessions with her divine Son.

Excitement filled our hearts as our bus wove its way around the mountains of Venezuela on our first journey to Betania. Trying to calm ourselves and prepare for the possibilities, we prayed a few Rosaries and enjoyed the splendor of the countryside. Before we knew it, we had arrived. Disembarking from the bus, we were struck by the beauty of the grotto and how it resembled Lourdes, even having a notch cut out of the mountainside with a statue of Our Lady of Lourdes standing within it. As at Lourdes, that area is behind an iron fence. There were thousands of flowers thrown over the fence and others placed on the fence as an offering of love to the Blessed Virgin Mary. Hundreds of candles burned there also.

To the left of the grotto area was a small waterfall. These were the waters that Maria said had been blessed, as are the waters of Lourdes in France. All of us let these waters wash over our heads while drinking from the falls copiously, praying all the while and asking Our Lady for healing of mind and body. We also took bottles of water home for later consumption. I said Mass at the open-air chapel, offering the Mass that day, as I did on all the other days of the trip, for the healing of Charlie and for the intentions of the other pilgrims. The chapel had a roof and floor, but no walls. It was wide open, perfect for the always warm-to-hot temperatures in Betania.

On many days of our pilgrimage, once breakfast was over and we had left the hotel in Caracas, we did not return until after dark. Lunch was purchased from local farmers who had stands on the mountain road just outside the gates to Betania. We were advised not to eat anything we could not peel first. Some obeyed Wendy's instructions and others took Imodium.

Many of our group saw a huge indigo butterfly leisurely flying around the property. Wendy said the blue butterfly was an external sign that the Blessed Mother was present there in Betania. I saw the butterfly once; it was huge, the size of a small bird, or maybe even larger. Those of us who witnessed the blue butterfly felt honored. It was not the same as seeing Our Lady, of course, but it was a consolation. At that point, who knew, maybe seeing the butterfly was a precursor to seeing the Mother of God at a later moment of our trip.

Some people on our pilgrimage did see the Virgin Mary. I did not. I saw the butterfly, but Our Lady I did not see. My parishioners asked why others had the visions of the Blessed Virgin Mary and why not me? If truth be told, if I had been graced to see Our Lady, I would have died of joy, and then Holy Mother Church would have had to find someone to take my place.

The final day of our pilgrimage, and the most grace-filled, found Charlie too ill to make the trip. So he and Mary Lou stayed at the hotel while the rest of us went off, around, up, and down the mountains to Betania.

Our Lady seems to work overtime to find out-of-the-way places to appear. For instance: Kabeho, Rwanda; Lourdes, France; LaSalette, France; Fatima, Portugal; all are way off the normal highways, and byways of the various countries. She must have a reason for her remote area appearances. Could it be that she needs to appear in remote paces because they are the only locations she can find people with a simple enough faith to accept and understand her heavenly messages?

Sometime after lunch, some of my fellow pilgrims witnessed an unusual but striking kiss of love from Our Lady. I must have been busy hearing confessions, because I did not hear even a whisper about it until we were on the way back, riding around those mountains again. A group from our bus was at the grotto praying the Rosary when they witnessed a large red rose glide, or float, down from heaven, landing within the fenced-off area. The Blessed Virgin appeared to some of these same pilgrims and told them, "That rose is for Charlie." Excited as they were, they could not retrieve the rose because it was behind the fence, so instead, they carried the lovely message to Charlie from the Blessed Mother themselves.

When the bus arrived back at the hotel, Mary Lou greeted me very excitedly and asked my opinion regarding something that had happened to her earlier during the day. She explained that she was sitting on the bed, next to Charlie and looking out the window. As she sat there praying for her good husband, she began to see images in the clouds. Mary Lou described it this way, "I looked out the window and started to see things in the clouds. It was sort of like a movie where scenes move across the screen; this time the framing of the window provided the screen. I saw in the clouds the Good Shepherd, then as he moved off the screen, the Sacred Heart appeared, and then the Holy Family. Mary Lou said, "All three of these were cloud formations of well-formed images. They did not stay stationary, but moved from left to right. It was all over in a minute or so, but it definitely made an impression on me."

I guess so! Who would not have been impressed? At that time I did not know why Mary Lou was blessed with those heavenly signs. However as the pilgrimage came to an end and life went back to normal I began to see the why of God's wisdom in the plenteous graces that flowed from our trip.

Charlie was not cured of the cancer. Some would say that our pilgrimage was fruitless because of the lack of a cure. They were wrong! Absolutely wrong! When Charlie arrived home his adult children were so amazed at the change that had occurred in him that they wanted to go to Betania and experience it for themselves. Charlie had changed from within. He had become very comfortable with the understanding that he was not to be cured. There was a peace and joy in his life I had not witnessed before. He knew God loved him and his future was secure in that love. He was given the grace to not only accept this fate but also to embrace the suffering that came from bone cancer, one of the most painful forms of that dreaded disease. To embrace the suffering meant that he had grown closer to Our Lord's own suffering on the cross. In the gospel of Luke, Jesus says to his disciples, ". . .if any man would come after me, let him deny himself and pick up his cross daily, and follow me" (Lk. 9–23). Padre Pio said that the more we suffer, the closer we are to Christ. Charlie was given the grace to do so. In the ninety-five days that Charlie had left on earth, he was given the grace to hold his newest grandchild and first granddaughter in his arms, to stand at a nephew's wedding reception to wish the new couple well, and to deliver a heartfelt tribute of what it means to have Christ as the center of a marriage. He also gave his extended family a splendid example of embracing God's will for him, and testified to the goodness of Gods love and mercy.

Sights and signs in clouds? That took a moment or two for me to process! My sister is a bright, simple lady. That is, her life is faith and family. She wanted nothing more than to be a good spouse and mother, and to live in harmony with God. She does not see abstractly. For Mary Lou to see distinct images in the clouds that day in Caracas was definitely out of the ordinary for her. It would be similar to me reading Saint Augustine's Confessions, in an evening and be able to grasp the depths the author meant to convey. Those things just do not happen.

I came to understand that for Mary Lou, those images in the clouds were extraordinary signs of God's love and goodness for her, signs to hold onto during the days when she had to let go of her life-long companion, her best friend. Mary Lou and Charlie had been married almost forty years. Throughout their entire marriage they would call each other several times daily simply to say, "I love you." The Sacred Heart and the Good Shepherd showed to Mary Lou Jesus' intimate love for her, while the Holy Family showed her where Charlie was being invited to come.

That is not the end of the story of my first pilgrimage to Betania. Once I was back in the parish, I would begin to cry every time I picked up a Rosary or drove by a church. I would not be thinking of anything sad or depressing, the tears would just come. They were not tears of sadness. They were external signs of grace in my life. My only explanation for this grace was that the Blessed Mother wanted to say thank you to me simply because I was good to my brother-in-law. Tears are the way the body reacts when it is overloaded with grace. The influx is so overpowering that it does not know how else to react, at least that is my theory.

Grace was given to me to overcome a sin that had plagued me for decades. It simply ceased to be a problem for me after the trip. I did nothing to deserve this gift, nor did I pray to be relieved of it on the trip anymore than usual. It was removed, I believe, by the intercession of the Blessed Mother for doing an act of charity. I went to Betania to help others. That was the only reason for me. Nevertheless, because of this, I was rewarded with grace upon grace.

It is no wonder that the evil one did his damnedest to prevent the trip. And that was only the first of my five trips to Betania, all within a thirty-month period. In subsequent trips, I was to meet the visionary herself. To my surprise, she read my soul, and because of that gift I was able to overcome a spiritual weakness that I honestly had not known existed, even though it was having a negative effect on my life. So hold on, many more graces were to be given to me in Venezuela.

Charlie's children, all adults, were so energized by the interior change in their dad that they wanted me to arrange a pilgrimage to Betania for them. Additionally, my former pastor and numerous former parishioners were anxious to experience what I had experienced because of the changes they saw in me. So we set a date for early October of the same year, 1994. There were about forty of us on this trip, including family members. Unfortunately this was to be the opposite of the first trip for me. It was a trip from hell.

At the time I was suffering from anemia caused by a disease inherited from my maternal grandfather who, strange as it may sound, died of a nosebleed in a hospital at the age of forty. That sounds very primitive in these days, but it is not out of the question when dealing with this disease, even today. My hemoglobin count was under six whereas fifteen would be normal for an adult male. One major effect of low hemoglobin is extreme fatigue, thus making ordinary activities such as walking a couple of blocks very difficult. Low hemoglobin puts severe strain on the bodily organs, especially upon the heart.

In addition to this, the evil one was stirring the pot again. Wherever there is good, the devil is also there doing his nasty, beastly thing of trying to destroy the godly. As holy as I knew my former pastor to be, he was not a happy camper on the trip. Heaven only knows why. He was unhappy with the hotel and the food; he was crotchety the whole trip, especially towards me. It was something that had been stirred up by that dastardly creature from down below. And to top things off, Maria Esperanza was in New Jersey again! I had come back to Betania this time to seek her assistance in overcoming many personal health issues, but once again she was in the United States.

Our Savior said many times in scripture that we must embrace our crosses. If we want to be his disciples, we must pick up our crosses and carry them daily. It goes ten-fold for his priest. In priesthood, we act in the person of Christ. We are conformed to Christ not just through the sacraments but also to him through his redemptive suffering. The priest is conformed to Christ on the cross! That was my lesson from the second trip to Betania; no consolation, just his cross. Not being the saint that we are all called to be, I found this to be more than difficult. Learning is never easy.

Let me digress a bit with a few common threads and oddities that always seem to happen on pilgrimages. With all the pilgrimages that I have undertaken in the last twenty-four years, I always remind the group that it is just that, a pilgrimage, not a vacation, and hardships will be encountered. As in life, strange things occur, to the point that you may think you have somehow encountered the Twilight Zone.

Our hotel in Caracas was not a four-star, nor was it even a one-star. Rather, it seemed to be made especially for pilgrims, with some quirky and some downright disgusting qualities abounding. For instance, we were having the soup course for dinner one evening when a young lady, Charlie's daughter, fished a cockroach out of her soup. Even though it was disgusting, she said very calmly, "It's a pilgrimage and I must remember that," as she put her spoon down in the soup, not intending to pick it up again. The people at her table continued to eat their soup while commenting on how gross it was to have that happen. After the soup course, she reminded them that their soup came from the same pot back in the kitchen. Who had the last laugh?

At breakfast one morning, a pilgrim related the story that he woke up to find boiling water in the commode. What? Yes, the water in the bowl and tank was boiling! The water was so hot it melted all of the plastic parts in the tank. The hotel had to have a new commode installed. This oddity did not happen to anyone else that I know of, thank God. Twilight Zone? I am glad that they did not ask me if there was some kind of message in this.

This second pilgrimage to Betania was plagued by constant attacks from Satan. Having forty pilgrims on one bus would be difficult in itself, but this bus contained so many divergent personalities that simply getting them to travel together amicably was a task for a master diplomat.

Diplomat is a designation that no one has ever used to describe me.

Years after the trip I heard that a few of the pilgrims had a wonderful time, but I have had the distinct impression that many of the pilgrims were very disappointed they did not see Maria, because she was supposed to be the highlight of the trip. However, there were some who were satisfied that they had visited a site where the Blessed Mother physically appears, even if they did not have the privilege of seeing her.

On the way back to the hotel in Caracas, returning from our last bus trip to Betania, as we were going up and down and around those beautiful but pitifully poor mountains, Wendy said she had some good news for me. She came close to promising me that "Maria is always home in Betania for the feast of the Immaculate Conception," December 8, just under two months away.

Was I destined to come back to Betania a third time within one year? Yes, and the third time is always is the charmer, right? Indeed this was to be true for me. Not only was I finally going to meet Maria Esperanza, but I was to experience many healings for myself, including the healing from a hidden spiritual problem that stemmed from a distasteful encounter that occurred many years ago. It seems I had blocked the whole affair out of my mind simply to be able to function.

Sometimes God makes us jump through many hoops, for our benefit, of course, to perfect us in virtue. It is never easy, but it is absolutely necessary for our spiritual welfare. This was most true on this, my third pilgrimage to Betania. Consolations and joy were to replace the pain of the previous trip.

Often in life things never seem to go as planned, and this trip had its difficult and unexpected moments. We had been in Betania for three days, making the trip from

Caracas around those confounded mountains daily, having a good time, but not having any success in contacting Maria Esperanza. Now it was the last of our bus rides out to Betania and the end of my third trip to Venezuela, my third trip without seeing the visionary and healer. It was noon and there was no sign of Maria. Things were not looking up. Did this mean that the Blessed Mother did not want me to see Maria? It was the Solemnity of the Immaculate Conception. Would the Blessed Mother do me the favor I that had been asking of her, on this her feast day? I was hoping against hope. Did it mean that Our Lord did not want me to be healed? Did it mean that I might have to fly down to Venezuela a fourth time? I was too physically sick to think about such matters, and to make things worse, I was suffering from a fairly strong migraine; I would have rated it a six-point-five on scale of one to ten. My hopes had begun to dampen.

Suddenly I heard Wendy say that Maria was in the compound and she wanted to meet me. Finally! Alleluia! Wendy, her assistant, Joyce, and I were called to enter the compound, Maria's home within Betania itself. Maria had this oasis away from the crowds so she could recoup her energy, which was drained by the incessant crowds.

We were shown to some chairs on her porch while waiting for this momentous occasion. We could hear her voice as she was making her way to the porch, accompanied by her interpreter. Maria greeted us with a ready, genuine smile and a warm handshake. She and Wendy carried on a light conversation, as they had known one another for a few years. Then Wendy introduced me. Maria spoke very kindly acknowledging that she knew that this was my third trip, all the while appearing to be looking deeper at something within me. If I had not known better, I would have said that she was sizing me up, but as I was to discover, she was looking at my soul. She did have the gift of seeing and reading the souls of those with whom she came in contact.

After a few minutes, Maria abruptly announced to everyone that we were all to proceed up the hill to the outdoor chapel for Mass. I was hoping she was going to cure me of my ailments then, or that I would at least have had the opportunity for a more in-depth conversation with her, but no, it was off to the chapel and Mass. My migraine was getting worse!

I vested for mass as a concelebrant, and praise God for that because I did not have to do much besides be a good flowerpot. The celebrant was an American who was leading a pilgrimage from his parish. A little later in the bathroom, I saw him cleaning up while making comments that showed that he had doubts about Maria and the apparitions. That was not the image he projected in public. Shocked, I wondered why a person like that would even bother to come.

It was hot and muggy, and I was really suffering. I must have looked awful because, as I was seated for the readings and homily, pilgrims were offering me water. Several took turns trying to fan me so I could feel better. I did not ask anyone for help, but everyone just looked at me and knew that I needed help. I have to admit, I was very happy to see the end of the Mass. I thought that might be the signal for us to finally go to Maria's compound where she would then pray over me and maybe I would be miraculously healed.

But no! People surrounded Maria as if she was the biggest pop star ever. This display of need from the people reminded me of a basic truth in life: we all need help of one kind or another. We want and need a sign from God that he loves us. Maria offered us that sign. She seemed to us to provide a special connection between the divine and all of us. She was a magnet. Some people sought to touch her. Others needed that connection to heaven or just wanted to say hello, and still others were longing for a personal healing for themselves or for a family member back home. All was chaotic! I thought I was literally going to pass out and die right there on the spot! I was sick, getting sicker, and my migraine was very intense and getting worse, if that were possible.

Maria stationed herself in the sanctuary just in front of and to the right of the altar. She was speaking to someone who had major physical ailments. This conversation/prayer had gone on for a very long time when I decided to try to see Maria myself. I thought that if I could just get her attention, she would understand how sick I was feeling and would be able to do something for me.

Diagonally from Maria, I was positioned behind the altar and to the left. I was able to stick my head through the crowd, and that was about all. I saw her! Looking up and focusing her sight directly at me, she used the index finger of her right hand and pointed to me, then made a line in the air straight to her compound. Although she was in the middle of helping someone else, and we were at least forty feet apart with no chance of speaking to one another, she became aware of my presence and evidently of my pain and suffering. I had hope again! I could manage the pain for a little while longer. What an amazing, sensitive, and gifted human being she was.

After working with that one person, Maria stood up and began her trip down to her complex. It was to her compound that she had pointed, indicating that she was going to see me and work with me.

I took off my alb and made my way down to the gated entrance to her compound. There I waited, and waited, and waited some more. It was about 2:30 PM when she looked up at me and pointed to her house. Now the time just dragged and dragged. My head pounded and pounded, while my stomach and whole system felt way out of whack.

It took Maria over three hours to make the three hundred yard walk from the chapel to her compound. She took time with every person who needed her. Talk about exhausting! Some priests experience similar situations in the discharge of their duties. I did not appreciate this virtue in her at the time. All I could think about was my pain and how long it had been since she made that directional signal in the air.

At last I saw Maria with her husband, group, interpreter, and other family members coming closer. They walked right by my group of pilgrims and went into her compound. As she passed, she seemed oblivious to me or to anyone from my group. The gates locked behind her! Was this the way it was going to end? Third pilgrimage, third bus ride from Caracas to Betania on this pilgrimage, last time to see her, was this really the way it was going to end?

I was so sick! But I was unwilling to give up. I pictured the Divine Mercy in my mind, with the rays of red and white coming from the Heart of Jesus. With his hands raised in a priestly blessing, Jesus defeated death in the image, because he bore the wounds of the nails in his hands and feet and he had come through a locked door. These were all signs of his infinite love for mankind and of his mastery over nature. I refused to be defeated. I began to repeat the words written on the bottom of the image. "JESUS, I TRUST IN YOU." I repeated those words over and over and over. My pilgrims were also praying for me. Many of them were there assisting me in anyway possible.

About a half-hour after Maria and her entourage entered the compound, a member of the family came to the gate and announced that Maria had asked for Wendy, Joyce, and Fr. Lange to be admitted. "Thank you, Jesus!", I said to myself.

I felt as if I were in a twilight zone, sick as hell, tired, hungry, and stressed out to the max, and there I was walking back to Maria's porch seven hours after she had said, "Let's go to Mass."

Neither Maria nor I am bi-lingual. That meant that there would be no privacy, since everything had to be filtered through an interpreter. Besides, there must have been thirty people standing around Maria and me, not to mention those on my pilgrimage standing just on the outside of the compound, about fifty yards away. I found myself standing in the compound on her veranda, waiting for her to finish conversing with others. As she approached me she asked, "What can I do for you, Padre?" I responded by speaking about my chronic and dangerous nosebleeds, and also about my chronic debilitating migraines.

A hereditary disease known as Hereditary Hemorrhagic Telanglectasia (HHT) causes my nose bleeds. The disease is rare but nasty. It kills one in ten and complicates life for most of the rest of us who have the disease. Most of my family is affected and four in my family, grandfather, two sisters, and a niece, have died from its progressive attacks.

Migraines have plagued me for over thirty years, and for about the past twenty years, they have averaged about eighteen per month. They are a severe hindrance to my functioning as a priest. At the time of my meeting with Maria, pharmaceutical drugs such as Sumatriptan (Imetrex) and Eletriptan (Relpax) had not come on the market. About the only treatment offered to a migraine sufferer was painkillers, which did not help me, but only made me groggy.

Maria ignored my statements about my chronic ailments and proceeded to tell me that I had a spiritual block. She explained it as something very personal and traumatic which had happened to me five years earlier. She even described the perpetrator involved, telling of his huge belly, and she mimicked his walk.

When Maria stated that I had a spiritual block and strongly suggested that I call it to mind, I almost felt as is she were playing a game with me. I was so sick from the migraine and weak from being anemic that I could hardly think, much less call to mind something that had been suppressed for years.

Then Maria said, "No, it was ten years ago." There! A light went on in my head and I remembered the incident to which she was referring. I had been a seminarian at the time. The episode happened on the first night of a trip to Jerusalem with a priest friend whom I had known since grade school. I was thirty-nine years old at the time of our trip.

We had just arrived at our hotel and had finished unpacking. I turned and looked out of the window for a minute or two. Father called me. I turned around and there he was sitting on a chair, undressed and inviting me to join in some sexual activity. I said nothing but turned back to the window and kept my eyes glued to whatever was in view. I do remember asking Our Lord for assistance. I finally heard the priest close the bathroom door, and then the welcome sound of the water in the shower. That was the end of that.

Nothing was ever said about the incident then or during the rest of the fourteen-day trip. To his credit, the priest went to confession when we arrived in Rome. I remember him coming out of the confessional looking as if he had been beaten up. I had already blocked out the event to the point that it did not register why he might look like that after a confession. A few years later he made an apology during a wake service being held for my Aunt. He looked directly at me and spoke about brokenness and how we regret many things we do in life, all while he was conducting the service. This had nothing to do with my aunt; she was a very pious woman, a good wife and mother. He was apologizing to me as he was leading the wake service.

Maria saw the whole event. I don't know if she saw it written on my soul, or as a movie, but however it was revealed to her, she had the details down pat. As she coaxed me, reminding me of the details to help recall the event, she was very gentle and spoke very low and with a great concern. She said again that it was most personal and disturbing. What a gift she had! The sexual approach happened to me in Jerusalem in 1984, and here I was in Betania, Venezuela, in 1994. The only people who knew anything of it were the priest perpetrator and one close friend to whom I confided. And now, through the grace of God, Maria exposed the whole thing so that I could be healed and move on.

I did not realize it until then, but that event with the priest caused me to have poor relationships with all priests. I had trusted this man with my life. Through his brokenness, my trust in him, and by extension in all priests, had been shattered. I trusted no one. Thanks to Maria, that was removed, and I began to have more trust in my brother priests.

Immediately after Maria read my soul, she asked me what else she could she do for me. I explained about the nose bleeding. All of a sudden it was apparent that she physically felt my weakened condition caused by the anemia. While standing just a foot or two directly in front of me, she took her right hand and held her palm parallel to my body. Slowly she moved her hand from the bottom of my feet, still parallel to my body, but not touching me, and raised it slowly, up the length of my legs to the trunk, then to my neck and head. Once she got to the top of my head she turned her palm to face her body and brought it down as low as her nose.

Everyone said that when her hand reached my neck and head, my complexion went from a pale, pasty white to rosy pink. Maria went over to the edge of the porch and spat something out. She came directly back to me and told me that blood was flowing into parts of my body at a renewed strength. She told me, "You have been given an extension of life." Maria then became animated, elated, and began to smile and sing praises to Our Lord, clapping her hands as others joined her in the singing. After a few minutes she came back to me and lightheartedly asked, "Anything else, Padre?"

I told her of my migraines and as before, she assumed my pain. She alternately lowered her head in prayer and then raised her eyes and head to heaven. After what seemed to be a few minutes she left the veranda, walked over to a grassy area, and vomited.

As I watched all of this, it occurred to me that she had assumed my illnesses and they made her seriously, physically sick. First I caused her to spit something vile from her mouth, then vomit! I did not like doing that to this sweet woman. The episode continued.

Once again Maria approached me when suddenly an external sign of the stigmata appeared on her left palm. Right in front of my eyes, a mark of Christ's crucifixion became visible. She asked for some ice to put on the mark of the Crucifixion. She winced in pain and looked very surprised. While looking up to heaven she asked, "Why, Lord?" I assume that she was communicating with Jesus. Then she lowered her glance from heaven and, while looking at me said: "Now I understand, this is a holy priest." (Maybe she should have asked one of my confessors about that.)

We headed back to Caracas. Still hurting a little from the residue of the headache and exhausted from all of the excitement of the wonderful encounter with Maria Esperanza, I was very much overwhelmed and stunned. It was midnight before we returned to the hotel. I did not go on any adventures the next day but stayed in the hotel and rested while my pilgrims went off to discover some more ways in which our precious Lord loved them.

Totally surprised, I had been clueless regarding the spiritual block. However, I was so glad to recognize it for what it was and to be healed from its effects. What a huge weight off of my shoulders! The human mind is so complicated. My mind had blocked out the encounter in order to survive, but to have it brought into the light, and to have the healing begin was worth all the trips, the inconveniences, the money, and all of the time spent. Absolutely!

Twice more on pilgrimages, I had the privilege of seeing and interacting with Maria Esperanza. My appreciation of her ministry and of her devotedness to Our Lord grew with each visit. On my last visit to Betania, Maria showed me a huge smile and said that she considered me to be a friend. I treasure that thought today, especially when I ask her intercession for current issues in my life.

Regarding the healing from the bleeding and migraines, I am sure that I did receive a healing, but it was not what I expected. To this day I still suffer from headaches as well as from the HHT.

There was a three-year old boy whom I witnessed being healed of spinal bifida through Maria. The total cure took three prayer sessions with Maria and I was present at the third session. When we left Betania, the boy was running around playing like any other three-year old. I would love to know how the young man is doing today, fifteen years after the miraculous healing.

Three specific messages from the apparitions in Betania come to mind. First of all, there is a definitive statement on the true presence of Our Lord in the eucharist, as was highlighted by the Eucharistic Miracle of December 8, 1991. Secondly, we need to love and be reconciled with all people. God loves all people, and wants each of us to see everyone, especially those in our own faith communities, as brothers and sisters. Thirdly, we need to forgive others, and not just bear with, but to accept, other people's brokenness.

Another message communicated in the apparitions at Betania emphasizes the benefits of asking the Mother of

God to be a part of our lives. Mary is an instrument of Our Lord to assist us in our hour of need, to give us hope and encouragement. She is a wonderful example of discipleship, of what we should aspire to become. Our Lady, our Mother, intercedes for her children, even when it costs her pain. She sacrifices for us, as we should for others.

Maria Esperanza illustrated what it is to be a disciple of Jesus Christ. She was loving and caring to all, taking time with the most wretched of people. She treated the lowly as if he or she were another Christ. She was generous, giving of herself in service daily to her Lord to the point of exhaustion. She was humble and most accepting of the cross of Christ. I am positive that her reward in heaven is great. I think she is a great intercessor.

Prayerful Thoughts and Images

The infinite love of God for his people is shown in more ways than we can ever express properly. Here are a few examples of his seemingly endless ways of reaching his beloved children.

The Image: A Crystal Goblet, Your Soul, and Sin.

Imagine an exquisitely designed crystal goblet filled to the brim with clear mountain water. The goblet is sitting in delightfully warm sunshine and the sun is being reflected in multiple colors off the intricacies of the cut glass.

Someone drops a large piece of dirty ice into the goblet. Immediately the water is displaced; it overflows. The remaining water is discolored and the sunlight does not show the detailed beauty of the glass any more.

The above analogy is a depiction of what occurs to our soul when we sin. The goblet is a symbol of our soul and the water is God's grace, his presence in our soul. When we sin, we drop the dirty ice into our soul. We displace God's grace and freeze his presence out of parts of our soul. If we hold anger, hatred, or a lack forgiveness toward someone, we hurt our relationship with our God.

Our anger does nothing to hurt the person with whom we are upset, but rather damages the covenant with the God who made us. Now, that is a silly position for us to take. Someone injures us and we allow that injury to harm our connection with God himself.

That is what sin does. It freezes God out of part of our soul, and if we sin mortally we freeze him out entirely. We can substitute any sin for the above example. Lust, covetousness, laziness, or pride would all create the same frozen state as our example of anger. Different sins produce the same results. They damage or destroy our covenant relationship with God, who redeemed us.

Maybe a concrete example would make the point clear to our hearts. Most of us priests are attached to our book collections or at least we older priests are, while the younger clergy make more use of e-readers and such. Most of us have had the experience of loaning books to people who never returned them. It might seem perfectly normal to hold a bit of resentment or anger towards the culprits who steal those books.

Purposely not returning those books is their sin; it is ice in their souls. It is a form of theft, and that sin hurts their relationship with God. Even so, why should their sins, their offenses against God, affect our relationship with God? If we hold onto the anger towards the culprits for not returning our books, then we have frozen God out of part of our souls. Silly! It is their sin of theft, yet we allow their sins to affect our eternal relationships with God? This does not make good sense, no matter what the sin.

We need to work always to melt the sins in our souls and seek to replace them with God's grace and his love, which prove his presence in our soul. In this way we become more like him. By consciously working to eliminate the sin in our souls, the ice begins to melt, and we are granted an increase of his divine presence. This, in turn, leads to his peace and joy here and now, and later, happiness in heaven, our eternal goal.

I have made many visits to the Blessed Sacrament simply to ask Our Lord to remove the ice from my soul. Troubled by the details of life, dealing with my own humanness and that of others, frustration, and an awareness of not being at peace with God, overwhelms my heart. So I just sit before him and try to let go of everything that blocks a deeper relationship with Our Lord. Sometimes I am able to picture the ice melting as I let go of daily problems. The longer I am able to sit with him, the more the ice melts.

The following prayer is based on the Sermon on the Mount which is found in the gospel of Saint Matthew. In the sermon we are told to forgive as our heavenly Father has forgiven us. Further, we are told to love our enemies and to pray for them. Many of us have a difficult time with these directives. The following prayer may be useful to you. The recitation of this prayer has helped to melt the accumulated ice in my soul.

Powerful Prayer of Forgiveness

Dear Heavenly Father, I beg you to forgive me those feelings that I have towards ____[name(s)]. Please bless them, and make me love them as you do. I ask all through Christ Our Lord. Amen.

We need to pray this little prayer as an act of the will even though the hurt or injury remains. God will take care of the rest. We should not dwell on the injury, which only helps the devil to stir things up anew, thus making things worse.

If we say this prayer several times a day, over time God's grace will soften our hearts towards whomever we are praying for. This becomes part of the method of melting the ice which blocks our relationship with God. The process is never ending; we always have sin and its effects, and we need to be vigilant in working to melt it away.

Hurts That Do Not Go Away

Sometime the hurt is so bad, so deep, that it will not go away. Opportunity knocks! We can offer the pain or injury as a prayer to God in thanksgiving for allowing us to suffer with him. I know this may be a bit hard, but Oh! the grace to be able to do so is so sweet.

Let's say you have experienced a nasty divorce. (Is there such a thing as a nice one?) The pain and anger are great in these cases, but as an act of the will, you can forgive, using the above formula. Then, through God's grace, you can accept the pain and suffering you have endured, and may still be enduring, and offer it up to Our Lord as a prayer to be used for whatever intention Our Lord may wish.

Just as Our Lord offered his pain and suffering for our salvation, we can offer ours, along with his, for the salvation of ourselves, for our family, for our former spouses, for an end to abortion, for the world, or for whatever holy objective we have in our hearts. This takes real love and a willingness to suffer, to suffer with and for Christ our Savior. Sounds challenging, but just think about how beautiful your goblet/soul will become. Through God's grace, what was a sin of not forgiving someone, of holding resentment, may become a prayer uniting you with the passion of Christ. Are you willing to give this a try?

An Unusual Experience of Grace

I do not know if the following image came to me from a dream or from prayer or maybe from my vivid imagination, but from whatever source, it struck me as illustrating a truth that others may benefit from.

This truth, understood properly, will help us better focus on pleasing Our Lord, rather than listening to the many distracting and contrary voices around us.

The experience: I had died and was surrounded by the purifying fires of God's love in purgatory. I had been dead for about three months when I became a fly on the wall while a family, whom I knew to be my friends and supporters while I was their pastor, were having their Sunday dinner. At the table were seated the husband, wife and one child, a boy about eight years old.

After saying Grace, the dad said something to the effect, "I sure miss Father Lange. He was straight forward, and you always knew where you stood with him." His wife chimed in with, "Yes, I liked him too, he was outspokenly pro-life." Without missing a beat the boy blurted out, "Yea, he was neat. Father always called me Turkey. Hey, Dad, pass me the potatoes, please."

The point I wish to make here is that I had made friends with the family, but three months after my "death," I had become a conversation subject at dinner and a fond memory. That was it! I was not a part of their lives any more.

The most important moment in my life had happened three months earlier when I "died" and met Jesus Christ face-to-face and experienced my particular judgment. It made no difference to Our Lord what opinions my friends had of me on that Day of Judgment. Only the truth of my lived life counted. When we will meet Our Lord and Savior, our eternal judge, we will go before him alone, naked, and without our support group. It only matters what Jesus Christ will think of us, of how we tried to live our lives in harmony with him, rather than pleasing family, friends, and parishioners.

The question Jesus will ask of me will be, "How have you tried to live your vocation that he gave you?" We all have vocations in life. Our primary vocation is to be a disciple of Jesus Christ; our sub-vocation would be how we actually work out that discipleship, through marriage, the single life, or maybe the religious life. The umbrella which is over all of these vocations is discipleship.

My eternal happiness, and yours, depends primarily upon our relationship with God, not with humans. Let none of us be misled by what others may think of us, but rather may we always strive to know the will of God. We must love one another, but first and always strive to be in harmony with our loving and merciful God.

How do we do the will of God? Daily prayer, frequent Mass,—weekdays too, if possible,—should all be part of our daily regime. Additionally, regular confessions and a heartfelt attitude that we always need to become better Christians than we are at present, and to be faithful to this program should be our number one priority.

Prayer to the Holy Spirit

Holy Spirit, please come into my heart,
So I may see the things of God.
Come into my mind,
So I may know the things of God.
Come into my soul,
So I may belong only to God.
Sanctify all that I think, do and say,
So that all will be for the glory of God. Amen.

In the coal mining regions of Pennsylvania and West Virginia, the stained glass in the churches has suffered greatly from the effects of decades of polluted air. You can walk into a church and not even glance at the windows because they have nothing to offer the beholder. The light hardly shines through them. They need a good cleaning.

The same is true for our souls. If we have an accumulation of sins, the sins block out God's presence, his eternal light of love. It becomes difficult to see our souls and the beauty that they once exhibited. When we are absolved of our sins in the confessional, all sins are forgiven, but a good deal of the residue of the sins remains. The effect of the sins, the scum, remains. The former attractiveness of our soul (the stained glass) still needs to be revealed. It needs cleaning, even after receiving the sacrament of Penance. Is this a shock?

If I tell a lie, it damages my soul so that the second lie is easier to tell. The third lie may even become effortless. Confession does forgive the sin, but the effect, the ability to lie with ease, remains. That ability to lie with ease is part of the dirt on the once bright and lovely stained glass of our soul. The soul needs constant cleansing. By frequent confessions, more of the remains of sin are removed. Other aids to cleaning the soul are frequent and worthy reception of Holy Communion, a daily prayer relationship with Our Lord, acts of charity, and alms-giving.

If we normally frequent confession twice a year, as many Catholics do, we honestly do not know how to confess our sins as God would like. More frequent confessions help Our Lord to shine his light into our souls so we can see the sins we had not noticed previously. More frequent confession means a more fine-looking soul. God's glorious light begins to shine into all corners of our souls and makes them sparkle with new life, light and glory.

Forgive and Forget

Saint Faustina approached her spiritual director and told him that Jesus wanted to have a picture painted according to the likeness in which he appeared to her. The priest, inspired by the Holy Spirit, recognized that he needed some discernment of spirit in this matter, so he requested Saint Faustina to ask Jesus a specific question the next time he appeared to her. The inquiry was this, "My spiritual director wants to know what the last mortal sin was that he confessed."

I could not imagine asking Jesus such a question. However, the next time Jesus appeared to Faustina, she asked him the question as her confessor had instructed her. What did Jesus answer? He said, "Tell him that I forgot." Can you believe that? The truth is that once Jesus forgives a sin, he puts the offense behind him. That is truth! It does make sense. When we speak of perfect love, a love that has no bounds, for him to be that generous would be natural. He is perfect love.

Yet we still allow our own pride and the devil, that nasty beast who lives down below, to keep us away from the confessional, and therefore away from a closer union with Jesus and a better life. Is it not time we begin to believe in the infinite love God has for each of us? Is it not time that we take advantage of the means of grace he has given us? The sacrament of Penance is a gift all Catholics need to take advantage of often, so we can grow into the Christians Jesus would like us to be.

Just how much does God love us? A couple of examples from creation may give us different glimpses and help us to wonder about it in ways as yet not realized. In his book, The Evidential Power of Beauty, Fr. Thomas Dubay looks at creation and how much time and energy our eternal Father has expended creating our world so that we may enjoy life on earth.

When we pick up a handful of sand from the beach, we hold around ten thousand particles! Yet, God has created more planets than there are particles of sand on all the beaches of earth. And we live on the only planet with human life, the only beings that are made in his image and likeness. How is that for love! How small we are in all of creation, yet how singly we have been blessed with God's attention. Fr. Dubay says that if Jupiter were one percent larger or smaller, we would not have life on Earth, as we know it. If we had no moon, the same applies. These examples and so much more show us that human life has been at the center of God's creation from the beginning. This is just one more incredible proof of God's abiding love for each human person.

The beauty of the earth is overpowering. We humans are the only occupants of earth able to appreciate his creation. Our Lord made all this just for us! A simple example may illustrate my point. If you have ever sat on a mountainside and watched a sunset, it can be breathtaking to behold. While watching the sunset, you may notice a few deer feeding on the grass or other vegetation. They don't look up to notice the beauty of the sunset. They are oblivious to anything other than what their instincts tell them. It is the same with all animals. We humans are given the gift of reflection, but animals are not.

We are most blessed, but in relation to creation, we are very small. We live on one of the smallest planets and we are some of the smallest of God's creatures. Yet we are important to him. We are the only creatures made in his image and likeness with intellect and will, with an immortal soul that never dies, except through sin.

Psalm VIII expresses this idea well indeed.

> O Lord our Lord: how admirable is thy name in the whole earth! For thy magnificence is elevated above the heavens.

Out of the mouth of infants and sucklings thou has perfected praise, because of thy enemies: that thou mayst destroy the enemy and the avenger.

For I will behold thy heavens, the works of thy fingers: the moon and the stars which thou hast founded.

What is man that thou art mindful of him? Or the son of man that thou visitest him?

Thou hast made him a little less than the angels: thou hast crowned him with glory and honor

And has set him over the works of thy hands.

Thou hast subjected all things under his feet: all sheep and oxen, moreover the beasts also of the fields.

The birds of the air, and the fishes of the sea that pass through the paths of the sea.

O Lord, our Lord: how admirable is thy name in all the earth!

Wisdom From Blessed Teresa of Calcutta

Blessed Teresa of Calcutta endured fifty years of darkness in which she experienced little or no spiritual consolation. Our Lord, for his reasons, hid his presence from this great saint of our times. Yet she is the one who gives us great advice when we are faced with discouragement, depression, or loss of hope.

If we knew, not just intellectually, but in our hearts, how much God loves each of us, then we would be able to rise above all of the difficult situations that we are faced with in life. Our Lord Jesus Christ is the love and steadfast rock who gives us resolute strength to carry our crosses and see life to the finish. We ourselves are the problem. We fail to see his love. We fail to understand that he is the rock.

Blessed Teresa has the answer. Her strong advice is to do serious meditation about Jesus on the cross, or Jesus in the crib. This was one of her secrets to faithfulness during those fifty years of darkness.

By meditation Mother Teresa does not mean that we should give the cross of Christ merely a passing thought or maybe a little head bow while saying, "Thank you, Lord." No. She advises us to place ourselves at the scene of either event, to be there, to smell the smells, to listen to the noises, and to look at the characters involved. Most of all, she wants us to pay attention to Christ, to understand who he is, and why he humbled himself to become man and to die on the cross. The events in these meditations are historical facts. By bringing them to the front of our mind to consider and appraise, we can begin to live in the reality of what they mean for each of us. After a while they begin to penetrate the heart and therefore give purpose to life, and to supply us with the understanding of God's goodness in both the good times and the difficult times. These meditations help to fill our souls with an infusion of life, of love, and of joy.

A Final Glimpse

There you have it: Windows Into The Life Of A Priest! Every priest could tell his own story, and this is part of mine. I share it with you for the honor and glory of our merciful God. I am convinced that my two mothers, biological and spiritual, are the reason why I survived my early life and have received more than abundant graces, not only to come back to the church, but also to be ordained a priest. The untiring love of these two ladies is why you are able to glimpse into these windows today. I am convinced that a mother's love is the closest mankind comes to the divine. Remember that, mothers! It is your strength, love, and example that keep your children on the right path.

Allow me to share one last grace-filled moment that I experienced with my mother, Thelma M. Lange. When she was eighty-four, Mother began experiencing transient ischemic attacks (TIAS). All the medicines available to help her at that time were also blood thinners. Having the bleeding disorder which runs in the family (HHT), it would have been a disaster for her try to take a them. So the TIAS continued.

The accumulation of TIAS took its toll on Mother. As time wore on, she became confused for long periods at a time, and when lucid she had difficulty translating her thoughts into words. She also suffered from diminished hearing, and from almost total blindness due to macular degeneration. She could not walk, was incontinent, and could not feed herself. Her head hung down almost to the tray of the wheelchair in which she perpetually sat. Faithless souls might say that her quality of life index was near zero. I had stopped letting her receive Holy Communion two years previous to her death because I never knew if she understood what was happening, nor was I comfortable with her ability to consume the precious host.

About six months before her death, while she was sitting in her wheelchair, I pulled her over to where I was sitting, and raised the front wheels of her wheelchair up off of the floor so that she had a chance to see me, and hopefully hear me. I was forehead to forehead with her, and spoke about who I was, and said that I wanted to give her Holy Communion. This monologue went on for a while as I repeated everything over and over.

I was beginning to get through to her, so I asked her again, "Mother, would you like to receive Jesus in Holy Communion?" She began to move her tongue around and I could see her trying to form words. She finally opened her mouth and in her pleasant soft voice said, "That would be nice."

My heart raced for joy! I was ecstatic! That was probably the first time I had communicated with her in over a year. Of particular importance to me was the fact that we did so over something which was so essential to both of us. I gave her the Blessed Sacrament and she began to cry. Tears flowed down those old cheeks. She knew at that moment she had received her Lord and Savior, Jesus Christ. That moment is indelibly etched in my memory. She was given the blessed grace to speak, to be coherent, and to understand the reality of the situation. She received Viaticum that day, as she did not receive the Eucharist again in this life.

Mom had always been a pillar of faith in our family. After my dad died she became the loving matriarch of a large extended Catholic family. Christ and the Blessed Mother were central to her daily life and because of that, our faith was important too.

When I was ten years old, my mother and my sister traveled to Canada to visit the shrines of Our Lady. I remember receiving a postcard from Mom with a beautiful picture of the Blessed Virgin on the front. Her written message was that she knew that I would love the card because of its image of Mary. Evidently I had a devotion to the Mother of God way back then. I still have that post-card on my refrigerator door. It's funny how some things just stick with you throughout life.

A few years after my ordination, I made the de Montfort thirty-three-day preparation for my consecration to the Virgin Mary. About fifteen years ago I was moved to renew my consecration to the Mother of God, not just annually, but daily. It became important for me to start my day by kneeling in front of Our Lady as depicted in an icon known as Our Lady of Tenderness. The Blessed Mother, being the most perfect of God's creatures, has a far better view of life than I. By this devotion and daily consecration, she has drawn me ever closer to her Immaculate Heart. I place at her feet everything in my life that might be meritorious: my prayers, good works, suffering, joys, struggles, pain, love, anxieties, fears, and more. I ask Mother Mary to keep me free from harm, and to form me into the priest her son Jesus would like. If God the Father loves Mary enough for her to become the mother of his only Son, then who am I not to trust in her loving care?

So began an invaluable part of my daily routine, which I continue with ever-deeper devotion to this day. Daily I remind Our Lady that I love her, thank her for her example, and for the constancy of her love. In my morning dialogue with Mary, I implore her assistance in matters that I know I cannot handle alone. Mother Mary always comes through for me. I love her and recognize that I am honored to be her adopted son. Just before ending my morning appointment with her by praying the Memorare, I remind her that I would be delighted if she would squeeze me into purgatory.

It was not until I started to meditate on a regular basis that I began to grasp the depth of God's presence in my life. From the tree that almost kept me from turning six years old, to the accident in front of the car at age twelve, to so many other blessings, too many to ever count, God has been in my life at every moment.

I am certain that if we decided to fully explore our memories through reflection and meditation, most of us would also see how many times we can point to God's hand being obviously present in our life. I have recalled these events of my life to inspire others to take time to recognize God's presence in theirs.

Psalm 137

I will praise thee, O lord, with my whole heart: for thou hast heard the words of my mouth. I will sing praise to thee in the sight of his angels: I will worship towards thy holy temple, and I will give glory to thy name.

For thy mercy, and for thy truth: for thou hast magnified thy holy name above all.

In what day soever I shall call upon thee, hear me: thou shall multiply strength in my soul. May all the kings of the earth give glory to thee: for they have heard all the words of thy mouth.

And let them sing in the ways of the Lord: for great is the glory of the Lord.

For the Lord is high, and looketh on the low: and the high he knoweth afar off.

If I shall walk in the midst of tribulation, thou wilt quicken me: and thou hast stretched forth thy hand against the wrath of my enemies: and thy right hand hath saved me.

The Lord will repay for me: thy mercy, O Lord, endureth for ever: O despise not the work of thy hands.

Whenever someone came through my office, whether it was for pre-Cana, funeral arrangements, Baptism, Confirmation interviews, marriage counseling, or whatever, I always asked one simple question. It was a question that I hoped would influence the rest of the conversation, and the rest of their lives. However I could see it in the people's eyes; they tried to read me and conform their answers to what they thought I would like to hear. Ninety-five percent answered wrongly, and over fifty percent had no clue as to the answer. We are grossly uneducated in this primary area of life.

The tough question was, "What is the purpose of life?"

I was astonished to hear the answers I received to this simple question here in the third millennium since the birth of Christ, especially in this materialistic culture of ours. I would hear, "To have fun," or "To use your talents," "To leave the world better than you found it," or "To be good." Many people were simply honest and said they had no clue as to the purpose of life.

Now that is sad indeed. We do not know why God created us? No wonder we live in a hedonistic society with high addiction rates of sex, drugs, greed, violence, etc. If society only knew and understood that the Creator of everything, the all-powerful God, truly loves each and every one of us and wants each of us to live with him in heaven, it would make life much easier, less complicated, and more joyful.

Oh, the answer to the question, "What is the purpose of life?" It is to get to heaven! It is that uncomplicated and beautiful. We are made in God's image and likeness, with an immortal soul that God created, so we can spend eternity at his banquet table.

The longing of the human heart tells us the same thing. Saint Augustine sums it up in his Confessions, when he said, "Late have I loved you, O Beauty ever ancient, ever new, late have I have loved you! In my unloveliness I plunged into the lovely things, which you created. You were with me, but I was not with you. Created things kept me from you; yet if they had not been in you they would have not been at all."

Blessed John Newman, the nineteenth century Anglican convert to the Catholic faith said, "To be steeped in history is to cease to be protestant." How can any human institution exist for two thousand years and continue to be faithful to its teaching in faith and morals? It cannot. The Catholic church is human and divine! This is the only answer. Jesus himself said that his church would be here until his second coming. And it will.

If the purpose of life is to attain heaven, then the purpose of the church is to help us achieve this goal. This is why Jesus left us the seven sacraments, a continuation of his ministry on earth, and the priesthood to administer them. It follows that the purpose of priesthood is the same, to get us to heaven.

Yes, my vocation is to administer the sacraments of the church, to preach the gospel message, and to bring people to Christ. Another way of saying this would be that my job description is to take your hand and put it into the hand of Jesus so it does not slip out.

How is that for a vocation! You should always be able to count on a Catholic priest to help you approach Our Lord, to straighten things out between you and God, and to draw you closer to heaven, your eternal home. Jesus did not create his priesthood for priests to judge or pick on you, or to make your life difficult. No, our vocation, by acting in the person of Christ, is to carry on his mission on earth by proclaiming the Kingdom of God through word and deed. Once more, our goal in life, our vocation, is to take your hand and to place it into the hand of Jesus so it never slips out.

"The Priest . . . is something transcendent: through Baptism he brings souls to birth, through the sacrament of Penance he purifies them, through Communion he gives them Our Lord's body as he himself did at the last supper, and at their death he helps them to appear before the beloved by giving them.... their final forgiveness and their supreme strength . . . Every single day of his life, he does what Jesus did during his years of ministry—he teaches men to know, love and serve their good Master. What a vocation!" (Charles de Foucauld—From a letter to a young friend preparing for ordination, 1897).

Appendix

Divine Mercy?

The motorcycle rider hardly knew what hit him that August afternoon. He was dead before his body hit the ground. So fast and so suddenly, life for him went from being one big party to death and to an unprepared-for meeting with the eternal judge.

Tragically, I watched my best friend die almost instantly in that motorcycle accident. That Saturday three bikers, Paul (not his real name), another friend, and I, were enjoying life in the fast lane, on the wide and dangerous road to hell. No thought crossed our minds as to the eternal consequences of our partying lifestyle, as we drank and smoked our way to oblivion.

We had been traveling on a tract of land owned by the government, which was clearly marked with a Do Not Trespass sign. Two of us had parked our bikes on the side of the road, ready to party some more. Our friend Paul passed us on his bike with the intention of circling back to join us in one last round of indulgences before we all headed our separate ways. That is what we had planned, but it was not to be. Our Lord had something else in mind.

As my buddy passed us riding his motorcycle he glanced at us, laughed, and then turned to notice a wire crossing the road no more than a few feet in front of him, way too close for him to be able to react.

The wire hit him chest-high, then bounced up to his neck. The force of the impact threw this 250 pound man to the ground and broke his neck in less time that it took to say a foul four-letter cuss word. Objectively, Paul should have gone straight to hell. He was a non-practicing protestant who embraced a pleasure-filled life with apparently no thought of the consequences.

My re-entry into the Catholic church was about two-and-a-half years after Paul's death. Once I reverted back to my faith, I began to realize more deeply my responsibilities as a Christian. Therefore I began to pray daily for Paul's soul. Recognizing also that I may have had a part to play in his death, my prayers for his soul became more intense as the years passed. The accident occurred in 1974. Eight years later, when I entered the seminary, my prayers continued for Paul even though I knew in all reasonableness that he should be in hell for all eternity.

Only God knows the full stories of our souls and the extent of his mercy, while the rest of us have our own ideas, suppositions, and theories. However, there is always hope, even for those whose lives seem to be directly opposed to the virtuous lives God would have us choose.

Being ordained in 1986, I began a daily practice of remembering my motorcycle-riding buddy at every Mass I celebrated. I never failed to pray for Paul. I held onto hope.

Towards the end of my third year of priesthood, I was on a private retreat in my family's mountain cabin. I remember a particular moment as if it only happened yesterday. It was this. I was sitting on the deck, concentrating on praying the Divine Office when I heard a motorcycle pass by the cottage. It was the first time I had ever heard a motorcycle on that mountainside. Instantaneously I thought of my friend Paul, and instantly again, I heard a voice inside of me which said, "I am okay, thanks to your prayers."

Our Lord Jesus Christ, in his Divine Mercy apparitions to Saint Faustina, indicated that, as a soul is falling into hell, he is there beside it, saying that he could still change things if the soul would only choose him. This indeed supports my understanding as to what happened to Paul when his body hit the wire crossing the road that fateful day.

God is beyond time. Our Lord, in his Divine Mercy, is able to reach out to a misdirected soul and offer it one more chance to be redeemed. In Saint Faustina's Diary, Divine Mercy in My Soul, Our Lord indicates more than a few times that his heart aches to be able to pour out his mercy upon even the most horrendous sinners.

As far as my heart is concerned, I have experienced two locutions in my lifetime. The first provided me with a definitive call to priesthood, and the second told me that my prayers of fifteen years for a friend were heard and answered.

I do not claim to know with positive assurance that my friend Paul is with Our Lord in heaven, rather that my locution (if that is what I experienced while praying the Divine Office) and the message from the Divine Mercy revelations fit together perfectly. I still pray for my friend, as I still pray for each of my deceased family members who, while still on earth, tried to live good and holy lives pleasing to Our Lord.

We should not depend upon our feelings, but on the eternal word of God in sacred scripture, as well as in sacred tradition. Our Catholic faith has always recommended prayers for the deceased, no matter how holy or needy we believe the deceased person may have been. Always follow our church in her teachings, rather than relying on your own assessment of a situation.

My opinion is that Our Lord, whose nature is love, brings each of us to our particular judgment at the optimum moment for the salvation of our souls. This is most important for those of us who do not live the lives that he would prefer for us. God is not constrained by time or space or anything else; therefore he knows what our lives would be if we continued on life's journey.

This is why, in my estimation, Paul died that day on his motorcycle. He was not a bad person in the sense of being hateful, belligerent, mean, or arrogant. He was not a thief and, as far as he knew, he did not cause anyone physical harm. Nevertheless, I am convinced that if Paul had continued to live the life that he and I were living that ill-fated day thirty-eight years ago, he would have continued down the hell-bound road to eternal destruction. Our Lord saved him from that and snatched him from the unending tortures of hell by bringing Paul in front of his eternal judge while there was still a little good in him left to salvage.

My faith is with Christ and his church. My opinion is just that, my heartfelt opinion. I live by my faith, and I express my opinions about matters on which our church has not defined its position.

For a better understanding of these opinions and to give substance for your hope, I heartily recommend a thoughtful reading of Divine Mercy in My Soul. Now are the days of Divine Mercy, before the time of Divine Justice.

This is a photograph of the tree that crashed onto the swing set in which Fr. Lange, then five years of age, had been swinging. His mother removed him from the swing less than thrity seconds prior to the tree crashing to the ground. The photograph was taken several days after the occurrence. Note that the swings themselves have been removed, and that the ground around the swings has been cleared of debris, thus not showing the full extent of this life-threatening occurence.

ABOVE: A miraculous incident! The circled portion of the hood ornament caught hold of the author's arm and held him off the ground until the car came to a stop.

This photograph is of Maria Esperanza and Fr. Lange during a meeting in Betania in 1995. Notice the unusual "light" in front of Maria and the white "hat" on Fr. Lange's head. The "hat" is not material, but rather, according to Father, an outwrd manifestation of God's presence (the Holy Spirit?). Note that Maria is looking at the "hat" rather than at Fr. Lange. Maria's cause for canonization is progressing.

A Eucharistic Miracle?

This photograph is of Fr. Lange's former home in the Shenandoah Valley of Virginia. It was taken during the first week after his bishop had granted him permission to reserve the Blessed Sacrament in his home.

A gardener working on a neighbor's yard noticed a very bright light emanating from the window of the home down the hill from where she was working. Her reaction was to snap a picture of the "strange" light. She says that it was so bright that she had a most difficult time focusing the camera. (She was not Catholic and possessed no knowledge of the Eucharist or of it being in my home that day.)

The light, in the shape of the Star of David, is coming from the window in the chapel where the Eucharist was reserved. Note that it was a cloudy day with no sun. I was at home (notice truck) but I did not have a light on in that window.

It is the opinion of the author that the light is a result of a Eucharistic miracle—God allowing his presence to be recognized in the most Blessed Sacrament.

A Eucharistic Miracle!

The Bleeding Host Miracle occured in Betania, Venezuela on December 8th, 1991. Just prior to the priest receiving the Eucharist at Mass, the celebrant had broken the large host into four pieces. He took one piece for his consumption and placed the remaining portions on the paten on the altar. When he looked down at the remaining pieces of the Host, to his amazement he saw a red substance coming out of it as if it were spurting from a wound. He placed the Host in a chalice and put it in the tabernacle until the next morning. When he looked at it again, it was still bleeding. Bishop Ricardo of Los Teques was advised and he had the Host tested in Caracas. He was told that the red substance was in fact human blood, type A-positive. (God is with us until the end of the age.)

This is a recent photograph of Fr. Lange and a friendly acolyte caught in a moment of joy after celebrating Mass for the Little Sisters of the Poor in Richmond, VA.